Creative COLOUR
Schemes For Your Home

First published in the United Kingdom in 1996 by Hamlyn
an imprint of Reed International Books Ltd
Michelin House, 81 Fulham Road, London, SW3 6RB
and Auckland, Melbourne, Singapore and Toronto

ISBN 0 600 58998 6

Cover design by Senate

Cover photographs:
Front Cover Three stars on red background – Jan Baldwin/Options/Robert Harding; Round green table – Trevor Richards/Ideal Home/Robert Harding; Green paint swatch with paint and leaf – Steve Tanner/Eaglemoss; Detail of flooring – Elizabeth Whiting Associates; Yellow floral sofa – Martin Chaffer/Eaglemoss; *Front Flap* Blue glass bottles with towel – Graham Rae/Eaglemoss; *Back Cover* Yellow flowers in coloured bowl – Elizabeth Whiting Associates; Blue kitchen with open door – Abode; Detail of dining room with green walls and chair – Tim Imrie/Ideal Home/Robert Harding

Printed and bound in Hong Kong

HAMLYN

Guide to Creating Your Home

Creative

COLOUR

Schemes For Your Home

HAMLYN

CONTENTS

LIVING WITH COLOUR

With the help of a colour wheel, you can assess colour relationships and discover why a particular arrangement of colours works — or not — so that you can mix and match colours successfully and with confidence.

You live in a brilliantly colourful world, surrounded by a kaleidoscope of vibrant and subtle colours in nature, on films and television, in pictures, books and magazines. Why shouldn't the colours of the paints, papers, carpets and fabrics you use for decorating your home be equally joyful and stimulating?

Colour is certainly the most important factor in setting the domestic scene. Different combinations influence and create moods, seem to alter the proportions of a room and establish a specific period feel. On the whole, vivid, bold colours give a room a lively, youthful image while paler ones create a more restful setting.

When you start to put together a colour scheme, the choice of fabrics, paints, wallcoverings, flooring and accessories is vast. Take a deep breath and please yourself first. Remember that the use of all colour is based on a few simple rules which are clearly explained by the colour wheel.

All other colours are ultimately derived from the three bold primary colours, blue, yellow and red, together with black and white.

7

THE COLOUR WHEEL

The colour wheel is a traditional diagram of the relationship between various families of colours and throws light on the best ways of using your favourite colours.

The colours used in decorating come from the pigments and dyes which colour paints, stains and inks for printing wallcoverings, and dyes for colouring fibres that are woven into patterned fabrics.

These start out as a pure colour, or hue, on the colour wheel:

The three primary colours are red, blue and yellow. All other colours can be produced by combinations of these, plus black or white.

Three secondary colours are obtained by mixing equal amounts of two primary colours: blue and yellow give green; yellow and red produce orange; red and blue result in purple.

SETTING THE MOOD

When you look at the colour wheel, you will see that the colours naturally fall into two sides: warm colours – the reds, yellows and oranges and their various shades, tints and tones – as opposed to cool blues, greens and violets.

Two colours come on the cusps – yellowy green and violet. Some yellow-greens are warm, some are cool, depending on how close the colour is to yellow or green. Similarly, some violets are warm, if they have a high percentage of red in their makeup; others can be cool as they veer towards blue.

▼ *The cool colours*

The colours on the blue-green side of the colour wheel appear to go away from you, making an area look more spacious. The darker shades and tones are less space-making, so use pale values if you are trying to enlarge a small space. They can also be used to fade an unattractive feature into the background. As these colours can make a place feel decidedly chilly, it is best to reserve them for a sunny bedroom like this.

▲ The warm colours
The reds, oranges and yellows from the warm side of the colour wheel seem to advance towards you, making a space look smaller and more intimate. They can also be used to draw attention to an attractive feature, but if overdone this can be overpowering. In a small space like this bedroom, use the pale tints of these colours if you want to warm it up without making it feel too enclosed.

The practical colour wheel
Decorating a room is similar to colouring up a sketch of the layout on a sheet of white paper. In reality, when it comes to choosing colour schemes, most people favour either paler tints – achieved by mixing bright primary colours into white – or muted and pastel shades and tones, obtained by combining primaries and secondaries together with each other and with various proportions of black and white.

Harmonious Schemes

Colour schemes based on a single colour, or a limited range of colours adjacent to one another on the colour wheel, are fundamentally safe and comfortable to live with. The ease with which they can be put together more than makes up for their lack of contrast.

Monochromatic schemes are the simplest kind of harmony, relying on arrangements based on shades and tones of one colour in a room.

These are virtually foolproof colour schemes which share many of the restful qualities of a neutral scheme, because the colours blend so well together.

To make them work successfully, you must make sure they come from the same basic hue. One of the easiest ways of building up such a scheme is to pick your colours from paint colour charts or tinted systems of mixing paints, where colours are arranged in strips of different tones and shades of the same colour.

Adjacent or **related harmonies** are made up from groups of colours that lie next to each other on the colour wheel. Look, for example, at the colours between blue and yellow and you will find a smooth transition from blue-greens and green-blues that is naturally easy on the eye. You can blend two, three or four neighbouring sections – all warm, all cool or a mixture of both – to compose colour harmonies that are very relaxing. You can see this cool-warm harmonizing put into practice very successfully in the yellow-green colour scheme of the living room below.

Contrasting Schemes

These are the dynamic colour schemes to go for when you want plenty of visual excitement in your surroundings. Calmness is all very well in a bedroom or living room, but a dining room, hallway, playroom or kitchen can often benefit from a more energetic look.

If you use the two colours diagonally opposite each other on the colour wheel together – red versus green, yellow against violet, blue with orange – you end up with highly stimulating schemes. By mixing warm, advancing and cool, receding colours, the association is never dull.

Their special relationship means that when used together, they bring out the best in one another. Red used with green, for instance, has more punch than it has when used with more harmonious partners.

For a vivid, high-contrast scheme, look to blending the brightest shades. Some truly enjoyable colour schemes can be devised around the less strident contrast pairs, like the olive green working so powerfully with the deep magenta in the bathroom on the right.

NEUTRAL COLOURS

Neutral colours don't appear on the colour wheel. But these non-colours are exceedingly useful either as an undemonstrative background for other strong colours in a wallcovering or fabric, or as a trim to define a specific design feature, like the woodwork in a room or on a frame round a picture.

True neutrals Strictly speaking there are only three true neutrals – black, white and grey, made by mixing black and white together.

Accepted neutrals Colours like the beiges, creams, mushrooms and tinted greys are commonly referred to and treated as neutral shades in decorating. They all relate back to an original hue on the colour wheel via the addition of some white and/or some black.

Other accepted neutrals are the very pale tinted or natural whites, which feature prominently in current paint ranges. Again these always stem from a pure colour on the colour wheel.

Contrary to common expectation, all true and accepted neutrals require extremely careful colour matching.

◢ The ultimate contrast
Paradoxically, without black and white it would be a far less colourful world. In combination with pure colours, they are responsible for producing a bonanza of the subtle and delicate shades, tints and tones that are so popular and familiar in home decorating.

In their own right, too, black and white are important decorating colours. Used separately or in exclusive partnership, black and white are responsible for some of the most extreme and stirring of contrast schemes.

◣ Treated as neutrals
Natural colours like these creams, beiges and honey tones are commonly regarded as neutrals. Here they are used in a similar way to the black and white above, to provide a restrained background and warm detailing definition.

PLANNING A COLOUR SCHEME

*When redecorating a room, how do you incorporate existing features
into the new scheme, and blend all the separate elements
into a satisfying and good-looking whole?*

F ew of us have the luxury of being able to create a room from scratch. You may have something you still like a great deal, or be stuck with a major investment that you can't easily change – a sofa or a carpet, say – around which you have to plan. In fact, this existing feature can be turned to advantage, because it gives you a starting point from which to work.

Professional fabric designers are expert at handling colour, so if any of the existing features in the room are patterned, follow the example of the professional by making use of the colours in the pattern as a starting point for your scheme.

The colour scheme of the room shown overleaf is based on the upholstery fabric of the blue and yellow sofa photographed below. A pattern such as this can not only tell you which colours go well together but also suggest the proportions in which they can be used. For example, mid tones in a pattern are often ideal for the main areas of colour in a room, such as the carpet and wallcoverings, while strong, rich tones are best used sparingly as occasional accents.

COLOUR CUES

When you are planning to redecorate a room, use the colours in the pattern of an existing feature you intend to keep as the basis of the new scheme – it could be a sofa, a rug, curtains or even a collection of favourite ornaments. A pleasing pattern will tell you which colours go well together and can sometimes suggest the proportions in which they'll work best. The patterned upholstery fabric on the sofa featured here is the starting point for the scheme shown overleaf.

 LIGHT TONE – a *soft cream* is the backgound colour in the sofa. Use light tones for a crisp, fresh touch to a room.

MID TONES – the restful *blue, soft yellow* and *beige-brown* are all good choices for main areas of the room such as carpet or wallcovering. Mid tones are often a practical choice – not so light as to be difficult to keep clean, and not so dark as to overpower a scheme.

 **RICH TONES** – the *strong blue, golden yellow* and *forest green* would all work well as lively accent colours and could be used for lampshades, cushions and other accessories.

TAKE ONE SOFA

The room shown here was planned around a blue and yellow patterned sofa. As is often the case, it wasn't possible to match the existing print exactly, so a mix of plain colours and complementary patterns in the main tones was used, with strong blues and yellows providing accents on accessories.

Because the pattern on the sofa is fairly pronounced, a plain colour in fairly subtle mid tones works well as a relaxing backdrop on two other major elements in the room, the walls and the floor. The sponge-effect wallpaper adds depth without fuss and the rich but restful blue of the carpet helps draw the scheme together – the colour won't show every speck of dirt so is a practical choice for a family room with a door leading out to the garden.

TRYING OUT YOUR IDEAS

One way to avoid expensive mistakes when restyling a room is to try out your chosen colours and patterns by collecting samples, so that you can see how they work together. For good colour matches, first start with a sample from the fixture you can't change.

Remove the cover from a cushion or use an arm cover if your starting off point is a sofa, or take a colour photograph in daylight.

Now start collecting scraps of fabrics, wallpaper, carpets and so on, in the colours you want to combine with your existing feature. Take the samples with you when you go shopping; when new ideas spring to mind, check them against your samples.

Don't try to play safe by restricting yourself to only one colour in a range of tones. A room with light apricot walls, mid apricot cushions and chair covers and a dark apricot carpet may match perfectly, but it's also in danger of looking dull and flat.

If you want to mix and match colour and pattern, look at coordinated ranges of fabrics, papers and borders which work around one of the colours in your existing feature.

Once you have collected your samples, display them in the room for a few days, as close as possible to where they will eventually be used. See what they are like to live with, and check the effect in both natural and artificial light, before you make your final choice.

COLOUR AND PATTERN SAMPLES FOR THE ROOM

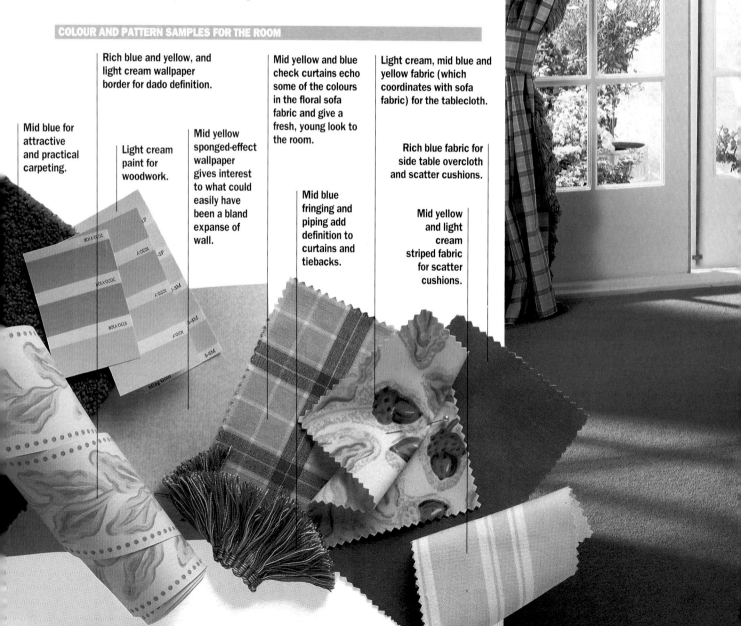

Mid blue for attractive and practical carpeting.

Rich blue and yellow, and light cream wallpaper border for dado definition.

Light cream paint for woodwork.

Mid yellow sponged-effect wallpaper gives interest to what could easily have been a bland expanse of wall.

Mid yellow and blue check curtains echo some of the colours in the floral sofa fabric and give a fresh, young look to the room.

Mid blue fringing and piping add definition to curtains and tiebacks.

Light cream, mid blue and yellow fabric (which coordinates with sofa fabric) for the tablecloth.

Rich blue fabric for side table overcloth and scatter cushions.

Mid yellow and light cream striped fabric for scatter cushions.

TAKE A DIFFERENT SOFA

Using a sofa again as a starting point for a redecorating scheme, here are two more ideas based on a plain colour and a simple striped upholstery fabric.

◪ Mixing patterns

Rather than playing safe and picking out a plain colour to match the striped sofa, a floral pattern is used at the windows and for accessories such as cushions, a lampshade and a tablecloth. The softly pretty scheme is worked around mid tones of grey-green and peach, with a light cream tone as the background.

◪ Plain and pattern

Capturing the right mood in a room is often more satisfying, and easier, than trying to match colours too precisely. With a coral sofa as a starting off point, the warm, welcoming feel to this room is reinforced by terracotta on walls and fireplace and the striped and floral patterned curtains.

Singing the Blues

As one of nature's favourite colours, blue conjures up visions of wide expanses of sea and sky. Decorating with shades of blue will bring the same exhilarating sense of space and airiness into your home.

A ll shades of blue – from deep midnight blue to palest aquamarine – are a joy to use in creating fresh, lively colour schemes for your home. Applying a lightish blue as the main colour theme over walls and floors makes rooms appear larger and cooler; simply adding touches of strong blues has a welcome cooling effect on a warm colour scheme.

Blue is a very atmospheric colour. By using different shades you can create many moods, from a refreshing bathroom to a calm bedroom, relaxing living room and sophisticated dining room. Most blues are tranquil, but in their brighter or deeper guises they can be vibrant and dramatic as well. A full-blast greeny blue like vivid turquoise dazzles while a dark navy impresses – both make daring accent colours to pep up a tame colour scheme.

Blues combine harmoniously with each other – and with most other colours, notably white – in a range of striking patterns, from bold checks and stripes to charming florals. You can mix these designs on fabrics, wallcoverings, tiles and china, confident that they'll look good together.

The crisp vivacity of bright blues with white is the perfect cool, clean alliance to use in decorating a kitchen.

MID-BLUE

The middle of the range blues are the true blues, between the richness of dark blue and the iciness of pale blue. These are the most familiar and versatile of the decorating blues – strong enough to contribute obvious colour to a room yet soft enough to be easy to live with.

When different blues are placed side by side, some seem warmer than others. This is because the slightly purplish and greenish shades have varying amounts of warming red or yellow in their make-up, while the more intense blues of the mid-blues are much cooler.

This makes a mid-blue just the colour to turn a sun-drenched room into a relaxing refuge. In colder climates, handle these cooler shades of blue with care because they can look harsh and chilly in weak sunlight. Save your use of icy blues for a light, sunny room or a warm kitchen where it will be appreciated. Introducing warmer shades of orange, pink or yellow into largely blue colour schemes also tones down their chilliness.

A fresh shade of mid-blue and brilliant white is a traditional combination which is always outstanding in paintwork or patterns.

◹ A blues medley
Mingling different shades of blue makes for adventurous and successful pattern mixing. Here, the cushion and blanket coordinate with the bedlinen and accent the background shade.

◮ Country blues
In this hallway, the arrangement of a traditional floral and modern checked fabrics against lavender blue walls relies upon the natural harmony of a range of blues for its appealing freshness.

◲ Come clean
For the cleanest, freshest colour combination, any shade of blue works well against brilliant white.

▲ Pattern as colour
From a distance, a fine navy check on the walls and upholstery in this comfortable living room looks like a sophisticated plain grey-blue.

▼ Calming effect
Pale, greyish blue is a particularly elegant and soothing shade for decorating a bedroom.

LIGHT BLUE

Pale, pastel blues are soft, popular and easy to use in all types of home style. They are arrived at by adding white to intense blues. The more you add, the more the brilliance fades to delicate shades, and warmer colours are cooled.

Cool, pale colours appear to be further away from you than they really are. You can exploit this optical illusion to make any small room seem larger and airier; a chalky blue will make a little bedroom feel more spacious and relaxing.

Pale blues team up happily with white and other pastel shades, like sugar pinks, primrose and pistachio green. For a dainty pairing, mix pale blue and lemon yellow in various patterns with plain woodwork to create a restful atmosphere in a sunny living room. In a pretty country living room, pick out a wallpaper or fabric in these pale shades; there are plenty of floral, candy stripe and mini-print designs to choose from. Plan the rest of the room round the pattern, using plain, slightly deeper shades of the pastels on accessories and flooring.

Subdued, pale greyish blues have a muted country feel. Their subtlety and delicacy lend themselves to creating calm, elegant surroundings in a simply decorated living room.

DEEP BLUE

While mid-blues are predominantly cheering, and the pale blues are soothing and refined, the deeper shades of blue are either grand or shockingly vibrant.

At their most intense, they sparkle with the brilliance of royal blue. These summer sky blues are thrilling to use, especially over large areas of wall in a hallway, where they catch the eye even though they are only seen fleetingly.

The formal richness of dark blue paint or wallpaper is ideal for decorating a large dining room which is frequently used for entertaining. Accenting picture frames or tiebacks with a touch of gold makes the room look exceptionally elegant. For a more casual, ethnic look, paint the walls dark blue and lay kelims or rugs in rich brown and terracotta colours on polished floors.

An attractive but more discreet way of using deep blues is to highlight them in a pattern or as an accent colour on cushions or a single armchair. Limited quantities of bold blue paintwork on doors, window frames or panel mouldings produce dramatic effects. A front door painted in a dark royal blue against white walls looks exceedingly smart.

◀ **Join the navy**
Decorating this bathroom in equal proportions of navy blue and cream gives it a smart, nautical air.

◀ **Certainly blue**
Shades of blue lend themselves to safe colour and pattern blending. The intense chalky blue on these walls also makes the small landing seem roomier.

◀ **Show stoppers**
Use unmissable blue bottles and towels like these to perk up your bathroom scheme.

▶ **Dining in style**
This dining set up shows just how good deep blues look against natural wood and fibre matting.

▼ **Sea blue**
The brush work of colour washing brings subtlety and depth to a dark greeny blue.

▲ **Aqua flash**
Splashes of vibrant aqua paintwork add sensational zest to this bathroom.

AQUA

These are the most fascinating blues, hovering as they do in that intriguing no-man's-land between blue and green. Precise shades are hard to pin down, partly because they appear to change quite markedly with their surroundings. A 'sure-fire' blue can easily become a 'maybe' green depending on whether it is used beside an emerald green or royal blue background.

When devising a room scheme including these greenish blues, it's worth considering how they are affected by different lighting. Daylight makes a subtle greeny blue seem bluer, while under electric lighting it looks greener.

At their subtlest, these greeny blues, like duck egg blue, are remarkably restful colours. They create the ideal atmosphere to cool off rooms in hot climates, without being too bracing in cooler ones. Duck-egg colour walls make a superb background for every sort of natural material, like wood and fibre matting.

Any watery connections of the sea blues really come into their own in bathrooms. For a breezy, choppy sea look, mix aqua walls with loads of pure white paintwork and fittings. To get a more clinical effect, paint the walls white and jazz them up with snatches of bold aqua.

Snippets of reds, russets and apricots inject just the right degree of warmth into an aqua colour. These popular colour combinations turn up regularly in wallpaper and furnishing fabric patterns. Create your own designs by stencilling motifs in terracotta paint as a frieze round aqua coloured walls in a bathroom or living room.

Blue Medleys

Choosing your favourite colour schemes for your home is all about using colours that make you feel comfortable and relaxed. Blue makes that choice – and your life – much easier, because it goes so well with a whole rainbow of other colours. Remember, too, that within each colour there is a range of shades and tones to set against the blues, that gives you almost endless scope for personal colour scheming.

❖ **Blue and yellow** Virtually any blue will agree with virtually any yellow. It is a classic sun and sea combination that brings a cheerful atmosphere to any room. Their partnership is just as compatible when worked out in muted and pastel shades as it is in bolder versions.

❖ **Blue and red** The coolness of the blues pairs well with the warmth of red in harmonious colour schemes that give rich and vibrant results. The various shades have their favourite partners. While the greeny blues go particularly well with orange and terracotta shades in country style schemes, bright royal blues and scarlet together present a thoroughly modern image.

❖**Blue and green** Never let the old saying 'blue and green should never be seen, without a colour in between' deprive you of many exciting decorating themes. Especially successful modern colour schemes ally brilliant or dark blues with jade in a bathroom or kitchen.

◤ *Shades of summer*
Lots of blues in action with vibrant yellows and oranges smack of clear blue skies and perpetual sunshine.

◀ *Warm versus cool*
Cool blue benefits from the warming influence of a strong red pattern.

◣ *Natural partners*
A bowl of lemons supplies the perfect boost for most blues, while a bright turquoise offers a more lively contrast.

SUNNY YELLOWS

As the colour of sunshine and springtime, yellow has a powerful feel-good factor. Any shade will introduce a cheerful feeling of perpetual sunniness into your home, to warm a cold room and brighten a dark one.

Yellow is the flash of inspiration in many a successful decorating scheme. In fact, identifying a colour as yellow covers a huge range of sunny shades that bring zest and gaiety into your home.

On the colour charts yellows fall into three main groups: soft, pale shades like primrose and buttermilk are light and restful, ideal for creating a relaxed, traditional atmosphere; sharp citrus colours conjure up an exciting, jazzier look; brilliant,

singing yellows, mellow golds and muted ochres are radiant colours, suitable both for daring, here and now decorations or richer, formal room styles.

Such a diversity of yellows lends itself to colour theming through all the rooms in your home. When you decorate each room in a different yellow, you generate not only a variety of happy moods but also a feeling of harmony and spaciousness throughout, without becoming at all monotonous.

Whether it appears as a plain colour or in patterns, on fabrics, pottery or utensils, yellow is an uplifting colour with many applications round the home.

PALE YELLOW

When rich golden yellows containing a hint of red in their make up are mixed with white you end up with a selection of invaluable shades like buttermilk and clotted cream. These pastel yellows are frequently used as a mellow alternative to brilliant white when you want to warm up cool blues and jades, or provide a neutral background or smart trim for a broad spectrum of bright colours.

As with any colour, the way you perceive a particular shade of pale yellow will vary enormously according to the lighting conditions and the colours placed next to it. These shifting effects will influence where, how and with what other colours each shade is used to best advantage.

When a room is bathed in sunlight, for instance, its pale yellow walls may look fresh and bright, but on an overcast day the same colour can look quite washed out. Such a fickle shade might prove uncomfortably cool in a living room during the winter, but ideal in the heat of the kitchen or a warm climate.

A colour combination found in nature is a good starting point for planning a decorating scheme. Imagine the creamy yellow and soft pink of honeysuckle blossoms, that look so pretty together along the country roads, reworked into an attractive bedroom or living room colour scheme. Explore other popular pastel colours like apricot and blue that will also bring out the best in pale yellows, when used as paintwork or in fabric and wallpaper patterns.

The classic mix of pastel yellow with pale grey is exceptionally elegant and easy to live with. Team pale yellow walls with grey upholstery or carpet and grey-yellow patterned curtains and cushions for a relaxing scheme in a living room, bedroom or kitchen.

For a more aged look, use pastel yellows as a foil for terracotta or dark red. Colourwash the walls in a hall with a creamy yellow, then add a stencilled design in terracotta at dado level.

◀ *Mixed blessings*
Mixing shades of yellow together in a room creates a naturally coherent scheme. Putting a pale, creamy colour on these walls provides a versatile backdrop for the deeper and brighter yellows in the soft furnishing fabrics and fresh flower arrangements.

◄ Rise and shine

The warm and gentle tones of palest golden yellow – freshened up with lots of white in this bedroom – are a joy to wake up to every morning.

▷ Lemon balm

All yellows are sunny, but those tinged with blue are cooler than the rest. Here a sharpish lemony yellow is colourwashed on to the walls to take some heat out of the kitchen.

CITRUS YELLOW

Yellows with a hint of blue in them – lemon, primrose and acid yellow – have a slightly greenish tinge. These citrus shades are the coolest yellows with the most pizzazz. While the sharpness of lemon adds zest to white, grey or neutral colour scheme, primrose is a particularly good foil for all shades of purple, from pale lilacs to vibrant raspberry pinks. Choose a wallpaper or furnishing fabric in a pattern or floral print using this colour scheme and treat it as a background against which to arrange a riot of rosy pink and purple accessories.

▲ At the sharp end

A really tangy shade of citrus yellow livens up a potentially dark landing.

DEEP YELLOW

These yellows are a warm, spicy bunch, ranging from the soft richness of mustard and ochre to the glowing yellows of sunflowers and buttercups. With their reddish tinge, the deep yellows are the colours to turn to when you want a room to feel comforting and jolly.

Warm, darker coloured walls always appear to encroach into the room, making it seem smaller and cosier. You can take advantage of this effect to create a more intimate and friendly atmosphere in a large room by decorating it in a deep shade of golden yellow.

A successful colour scheme depends on balancing one colour with another. Placed next to red, a warm yellow can look even warmer. This is fine in winter, when you will enjoy the sensation of warmth, but might look rather hot in summer or the tropics. For a better balance, warm yellows relax beside white or a cool blue. A large expanse of blazing yellow backing a smaller area of a cool colour, or equal amounts of warm and cool against a background of white, works well.

Play down any tendency to brashness in the most vivid yellows by teaming them with the more subdued, cooler shades of lavender, jade or charcoal – the contrasts are most exciting.

To see what other colours go well with golden yellows, again take your lead from nature. Picture bright yellow buttercups bobbing above the lush green grass of a field with scarlet poppies and brilliant blue cornflowers nearby; corn ripening under a clear blue sky; or daisies wearing a halo of white petals round their yellow centres. Treat these scenes as inspiration for some lively, up-to-the-minute colour scheming.

On the whole, all the bright, deep shades of yellow have to be handled with care for fear of swamping neighbouring colours. These exuberant colours are at their best when used as small accent touches, because they catch the eye so readily.

◁ Bright lines
In this kitchen-cum-dining room, a golden wallpaper happily combines the exuberance of yellow with the elegance of regular stripes.

▷ A suntrap
Colourwashing these walls in a bright yellow leaves the whole room looking as though it is constantly flooded in dappled sunshine.

◁ Warming up
As deep yellows drift towards apricot and orange, they become warmer and warmer. Colours in this range harmonize well together in vibrant patterns.

◁ A golden rule
Like other deep, warm colours, bold yellows make a room appear smaller. Here, drenching the walls of a large living room in a rich, golden yellow creates quite a cosy feeling, in spite of its spaciousness. The warm yellow theme is carried through successfully to the carpet and upholstery, with the dark wooden furniture acting as a strong contrast.

ACCENTS

Using bright accent colours, such as the brassier and zingier yellows, is like inserting visual punctuation marks into your decorating scheme. Small areas of strong colour should stop you in your tracks as you scan the room and, by drawing your attention to an otherwise dull corner or blank space, add excitement to the whole arrangement.

An eagle eye for the smaller details of a room is also terribly important if the scheme is to sparkle with original-ity. Again the irresistible brightness of the boisterous yellows comes into its own as a refreshing accent. Normally, such intense shades have to be treated with respect to avoid them swamping the rest of the colour scheme. Used in small doses, however, to pick out wooden mouldings on a door, or add a vibrant tweak to the soft furnishings as cushions and lampshades, they shine out attractively.

Look out for bold yellow rugs, throws and ornaments as well and distribute them strategically round the room. In springtime, use the bril-liant yellows of daffodils and tulips in temporary displays, moving them to new positions in the room at whim.

▲ Sunspots
Dotted round the room like this, bright yellow flowers, vases and a throw unify a colour theme and attract attention independently too.

▲ Sunny side up
The sun is always shining in this bathroom, thanks to its yellow ceiling. It succeeds in warming up the cool whiteness of the tiles without intruding unduly on the overall colour scheme.

◄ The Midas touch
The pale yellow walls stand back and let the strong yellow upholstery take most of the credit for the inviting warmth of this elegant living room.

BLUE AND YELLOW

For upbeat colour schemes, blue and yellow are an infallible team.
A splurge of yellow here plus a smidgen of blue there – or vice versa – is the
basis of the jolliest patterns and decorations in any home.

Both blue and yellow are extremely variable and versatile colours in their own rights. While blues span an amazing range, from lavender to delicate duck-egg blue on the one hand and regal purple to brightest turquoise, yellows are equally widely spread from sharp, acidic greeny yellow to a rich, orangy gold. Consequently, it comes as no surprise that when you team them up together, the design possibilities just snowball.

Whichever way you juggle the cool airiness of blue with the warm optimism of yellow you come up with some outstandingly buoyant effects. Whether you put vibrant shades side by side, or plump for subtler, paler versions,

excitement and sophistication is guaranteed. However, probably the most successful pairings occur when the two colours are tonally similar. As the warm, advancing colour, yellow is often easier and cosier to use as the backdrop for blue floors, upholstery and paintwork, although there's nothing to stop you swapping the two colours round.

With such a broad palette of shades at your disposal, you can hit on a blue and yellow alliance to enhance any room style, from the bold and jazzy for a young apartment, soft modern or Mediterranean look to muted or pastel shades to suit a traditional cottage, town house or American country image.

The easy-going rapport between blue and yellow is an object lesson in colour tolerance. In this room, a golden yellow wall proves a congenial host to a whole range of blues, from the true blue of the chair and the pale blue in the picture frame to the purplish blue of the hydrangeas.

ON THE BRIGHT SIDE

Nature is full of good examples of blue and yellow teamed up successfully. When you follow suit and set the yellow of sunshine, daffodils and ripening corn against the royal blue of cloudless summer skies, cornflowers and the clearest oceans in your decorating, you're bound to end up with some pretty energizing effects.

Luminous blues and yellows are ideal for bringing a Mediterranean-style splash of bright colours to a kitchen. Colourwashed walls in layers of golden yellow have a rich depth of colour which is set off well by woodwork painted in a strong mid blue. Royal blue and white checked or Provençal patterned cotton fabrics for curtains, table cloths and chair covers add an authentic soft touch.

▲ Walking on water

As in many partnerships, one of the blue-and-yellow pairing outshines the other at times. In this bathroom, the sparkling royal blue floor tiles have a sensational impact. The primrose yellow walls are far from wasted, however, as they save the rest of the white-tiled room from looking chilly and clinical.

▲ Family fun

The designers of coordinated ranges of fabrics and wallpapers frequently exploit the natural compatability of blue and yellow. With their help, picking blue and yellow as the colour theme for a lively family room like this is virtually guaranteed to be successful.

◀ Fair and square

Bright blue and yellow is a popular and striking combination in many fabric designs.

▲ Local accents

Dashes of vibrant colour, like the deep royal blue and mustard yellow cushions on this settee, are brilliant at perking up the whole colour scheme.

▼ Backing yellow to warm up blue

Golden, colourwashed walls serve as a sunny backdrop for pools of deep blue in the fireplace and the sea-green blue of the furniture.

SOFTER SHADES

Pale yellows and blues possess a springtime freshness and vitality that lighten and brighten any room. In a sunny room you can get away with letting the cool blue predominate, but in a chilly room you might prefer to reverse the proportions and concentrate on yellow as the main colour on the walls.

Such delicate colours make a good choice for decorating a nursery. Muted blues and yellows also have a suitably watery and sunny connotations for a bathroom. The ever adaptable combination of yellow and blue is equally at home in a restful living room or bedroom.

Used with cool blues, pale yellow looks soft and warm. Faded blue-greens and golds are ideal for creating a traditional Scandinavian look.

▶ Scandinavian colours
Soft and muted blues and yellows are a classic part of the Scandinavian palate. They also make a happy warm, watery combination for decorating a bathroom.

◪ For a boy or a girl
Yellow is a jolly, non-committal colour for decorating a nursery, while blue fabrics, posters, soft toys and accessories supply the perfect rejoinder.

◀ *Cottage appeal*
It takes the right combination of colours as well as patterns to carry off a specific look successfully. Here, for example, a busily patterned duvet cover and sprigged floral wallpaper in restful, pale shades of blue and yellow capture the friendly, fresh nature of cottage style.

▼ *Yellow blueprints*
When you've hit on a magic colour formula in a fabric or wallpaper, you want to let it flow through the room. Sponging blue and yellow paint over the white walls in this bathroom is one way of making more of the winning colour combination in the bright blue and yellow curtain fabric.

◥ *Faded glory*
No matter how you mix them, blues and yellows turn up trumps. In this kitchen, the muted lavender blue tiles and blue-grey stained units strike up an interesting rapport with the mustard coloured tiles on the work surface.

LAVENDER BLUE AND YELLOW

When you remember from the colour wheel that yellow's complementary partner is purple, it's easy to understand why some of the most outstanding decorating effects result from mixing yellow with lavender or mauvish blues. The delicate colours of primroses and pale violets in the spring hedgerows, for example, translate into charmingly fresh room schemes.

◪ Grown-up together
Lavender blue-grey with yellow portrays the sophisticated face of blue and yellow in this luxurious bedroom. The plain areas of carpet, wall and fabric are perfectly complemented by the two colours together in the patterns on the bed drapes and the wallpaper over the dado.

◪ Spicy recipe
Soft mustard yellow mixed with different shades of lavender is an unexpected recipe for success – yet the resulting large-scale floral pattern is exotic and interesting.

◧ All aboard
For a very fresh and summery look, the palest yellow supplies an accommodating neutral background for an assortment of blues.

GREEN LIVING

Green is a lively, invigorating colour. Nature's favourite, it is a wonderful way of bringing a hint of fresh air and natural harmony into your home.

Green reflects all the splendour and freedom of open spaces in the countryside, of rich pastures and forest canopies. A fresh, invigorating colour, it brings a sense of the outdoors indoors wherever you use it in your home.

From the grey-tinged greens of rosemary to the citric tones of lime, green has many guises that allow it to be either a restful colour or one with zest. The key to the many moods of green lies in its make-up. A secondary colour – formed by mixing yellow with blue – it ranges from turquoise, at the blue end of the colour wheel, to lime, an intense yellow green. Heavily weighted towards yellow, expect

a colour that has vibrancy and warmth. Move round towards the blues, and it will be cooler, even tranquil.

Add white or black and the range begins to resemble the myriad of choices on offer in nature itself. Grey greens are quietly sophisticated, while pale apple still retains the warmth and vibrancy of the intense true hue.

With this many options, the first consideration must be the mood you want to set – is it to be bright, using vivid greens, or tranquil using the soft shades? Whatever your decision, take assurance from the fact that green, in all forms, is easy on the eye – it is, after all, nature's neutral.

Flowers, fruits and vegetables enhance the natural overtones of an invitingly fresh green and white table setting. Checks and stripes make a crisp backdrop for patterned china in a variety of green shades.

THE SOFT OPTION

Strong blue-greens and vibrant yellow-greens can be softened by mixing them with white. The resulting shades can be used quite freely in your decorating scheme without being overwhelming. Subtle though they are, they can still create a definite atmosphere, especially when used liberally as background on walls.

As with pure greens, there is a pleasing range of soft greens to choose from. Yellow greens water down to reveal their yellow makeup even more – and will inject a sense of sun into a dark room. Blue greens, diluted with white, are fragile and fresh, and possibly the most tranquil choice of all.

At both ends of the spectrum, soft greens are versatile enough for every room in the home. Pair pale apple or lime with country, rustic style furnishings – the warmth of these greens, even at their palest, will blend pleasingly with the honey tones of wood. The coolness of pale turquoise, on the other hand, is a soothing choice for a bedroom or bathroom. The clarity of these bluey greens combines well with more streamlined, modern furnishings.

▷ *Tonal solution*
A warm apple green makes this room glow with colour. Using a range of greens plus white is a simple way of creating an effective scheme.

▲ *Living with green*
Soft greens are restful colours, ideal for living- or bedrooms. Here green is used to make a feature of the shelving as well as to pick out the moulding around the walls and on the door. This shade also serves to bring together differently patterned fabrics used for the carpet and upholstery.

▷ *Blowing hot and cold*
Green can have a warming or cooling effect depending on the amount of yellow or blue in its make-up, and the colours used with them. These fresh mint green walls have a bluish tinge which is heightened as much by the pale yellow bedlinen as the strong primary blue cushions and sidetable.

▶ Green peace
In its most diluted state, green provides a charmingly fresh accent in a pure white room. The delicate wallpaper pattern and pretty tab headed curtains in a soft grey green give this bedroom a feminine touch.

▼ Refreshingly cool
The subtlety of the grey-green walls is accentuated by the addition of the picture frames and mounts and towels in a stronger grey-green tone.

GREY GREENS

For subtle and sophisticated decorative schemes, reduce the strength of rich blue-greens by mixing them with grey instead of white. These tints work particularly well on walls, providing a versatile background for most furnishing styles. In a living room pale, smoky green on the walls counterpoints traditional style furniture to produce a refined, elegant look. In a modern setting, gentle grey green walls can soften stark or streamlined furnishings and temper modern fabrics featuring strong, complementary colours such as hot pinks, oranges or reds.

For a tranquil and soothing scheme, grey-green and cream are perfect partners. Use them as solid colours, or look for prints in the theme – when working with such reduced colours, it's perfectly safe to mix patterns and still retain a light airy feel. Alternatively, work in the reverse and use grey-green as an accent colour for woodwork and accessories, against cream or neutral walls.

DEEP GREENS

Deep clear greens, including forest, ivy, and bottle green, are strong, intense colours that work best in rooms with bright natural light where they can have a dramatic effect – in dim light, dark green fabric has a nasty habit of looking black. Arrange chairs or sofas covered in a deep green fabric in a sunny spot or under a pool of light cast by a table lamp. Balance dark green by partnering it with brilliant white or soft ivory painted skirting and window frames for a fresh, crisp effect. Deep green can also be tempered by combining it with natural light coloured wood.

Although greens have a reputation for being fresh country colours, there is a more sophisticated side to their characters. A rich jade green can look coolly cultured, ideal for a smart town house look. It also works well in a bathroom with natural wood or contrasting white fittings and perhaps mirrored cabinets to make the most of the light.

A deeper pine green is ideal for a formal room, but to create light and contrast introduce rich reflective surfaces, such as a mirror with a carved and gilded frame or brass candle sticks. This deep pine green also makes a splendid foil for a wide range of contrasting colours such as fuchsia or lilac, peach, coral or terracotta. The same green works well as an accent colour – it looks superb when used with pastels such as primrose yellow or pink.

◪ *Use your greens*
Pale wallpaper in a lighthearted design and smart green and white checked fabrics complement the deeper green tiles around the work surfaces. The highly glazed though dark tiles reflect rather than absorb the light.

◪ *Naturally restrained*
Colourwashed sea green walls provide a pleasing background in a well-lit bedroom. Light coloured wicker furniture and a wooden floor balance the dark green soft furnishings and reinforce the natural feel of the room.

INDOORS AND OUT

Green is the colour most frequently associated with gardens and landscapes – authentic leafy or mossy greens give the effect of bringing the outdoors inside. More literally, using authentic greens in a conservatory or room with large windows overlooking a garden has the effect of visually linking the two areas. Reinforce this effect by displaying lots of leafy or flowering pot plants inside. The plants will also serve to intensify the depth of greens in the room. The logical companion to these vivid leafy greens is furniture made from natural materials such as cane, wicker and timber, and, coincidentally, they are also perfect choices for garden settings. The ideal flooring would be polished wood or fibre matting.

▶ Natural selection
Plain or patterned china and pottery in warm green shades is ideal for pretty flower arrangements or for serving fresh fruit.

▼ Indoor gardening
Green paint for walls and upholstery looks perfect in a conservatory room, supplying a visual link between home and garden. Use green and white checked or striped fabric combined with fibre matting or quarry tiles on the floor. Pot plants are the essential finishing touch.

◀ Pine fresh
Deepest pine green works well when balanced by dazzling white. Here, the deep green wall colour is also lifted by a collection of framed prints and the pale verdigris chair.

VIBRANT GREENS

Vigorous and exuberant, acid lime and grass greens are a brave but rewarding choice for walls. For a really clean, dynamic look, partner these racy greens with sparkling white woodwork and fittings. Use them to dramatic effect in halls, cloakrooms, bathrooms and kitchens, by combining them with materials such as antique stained pine or dark wood, colours which absorb some of the brightness. Break up bold expanses of green wall with lots of pictures and ornaments. For a brilliant summery effect, complement bright green walls and fabrics with bright yellow accessories.

Vibrant greens can also look sensational when used in small amounts with other colours such as blues, purples and reds. Add lime green accessories like cushions and china to give a boost to spicy colour schemes in earthy colours such as russets and ochres or pinker schemes such as coral. The almost fluorescent quality of the sharpest greens can mean that a little goes a long way – a trim of acid green piping instantly adds zest to a cream and green sofa.

◤ Original zing
Green works equally well as a foil for both the colours from which it originates. Here, tangy yellow and jewel bright blue are used as accent colours in a gloriously summer-fresh dining room scheme.

◀ Perfect partners
Natural wicker and earthy terracotta coloured napkins heighten the impact of the vibrant walls and at the same time prevent the complete scheme from being too bright.

◢ On the tiles
This glowing mix of sea and leaf green tiles has a Mediterranean feel that would enliven any room.

◀ Zest for life
Deep blue-green teamed with sharp lemon yellow produces an exciting modern feel that's fun as well as stylish.

THINK PINK

Whether you use soft, feminine pinks to bring a sense of romance to your decorating, or flaunt thrilling shades of vibrant raspberry or coral in your home, pink is a versatile colour that adds warmth to any scheme.

C uriously, there is no such thing as pale red, light scarlet or pastel crimson. The softened tones and tints that result from mixing reds with white are distinctive enough to merit a special name in their own right – pink. From modestly blushing pinks to sultry coral, luscious raspberry and shocking pinks, there is a pink to appeal to all tastes and styles of decorating. Once dismissed as a sugary sweet colour, fit only for decorating little girls' bedrooms, a rethink on pink shows it to be a highly obliging colour, with many different shades to mix and harmonize.

Pinks basically come from the warm side of the colour wheel, and are an excellent way of introducing a welcome glow to any room that lacks light. The paler pinks are essentially feminine and pretty, while the more intense shades are dramatic and exciting. Subtle patterns in wallpapers, borders and fabrics, and a mixture of pink tones and textures in fabrics and carpets bring variety to one-colour schemes

Colourwashing a wall in a deep coral pink brings warmth and charm to its surroundings. Although a distinctive colour, it provides an obliging background for natural wooden furniture and ornaments.

WARM PINKS

The warmer tones of pink have a hint of orange or yellow in their make up. They range from the delicate, pale peachy pink of seashells to the yellowish pink of salmon, the browny pink of terracotta and the intense, orangey pink of exotic coral. In a confined area, a paler, peachy shade neutralizes coolness without making the room appear any smaller. You can reserve your use of the more intense, warmer pinks to creating a hospitable cosiness in a hallway or to brightening up a large, sunless room.

For a happy balance of warm and cool colours, unite shades of salmon and coral with white or cream – calico curtains or blinds against coral walls work beautifully together and convey a soft, modern image. Warm, terracotta pinks can also be teamed with cooler shades of greens and turquoise for an up-to-the-minute look.

SHELL PINKS

The lighter warm pinks are fun to use and a delight to live with. They add cosiness without dominating a scheme, creating a foil for many other colours. You can thaw the chilly atmosphere of cool bathrooms or cloakrooms with warm, shell pink walls. Or a pale, salmony pink makes a wonderful background for old timber, polished floorboards and country furniture.

Shell pinks find their true complementary shades in the pale, blue-greens, but also work well with the lighter shades of blue and lilac. Or try using the stronger versions of scarlet and crimson as accents. A pale, peachy pink fabric is a good choice for a sofa or living room curtains and tones well with a wide range of other pastel shades and patterns. You can team it with off-white walls for a warm, feminine room.

▲ *Room for all*
Warm coral pink walls provide a remarkably versatile background for a range of colour-coordinated patterns and smart wooden furniture.

◄ *A restful bedroom*
A blush of salmon pink looks far from little girlish in this elegant bedroom. The delicate colour provides a perfect background for fine, sheer curtains and dark wooden furniture.

 **The power of pattern**
Even a paler shade of pink can look imposing when it is used with white in broad, dramatic stripes.

CORAL PINKS

Coral pinks can live up to grand surroundings, teamed with dark wooden furniture, ornate gilded mirrors and the rich, earthy colours of oriental- style rugs. Cool the effect down with lots of white woodwork or break up the colour by using shades of coral pink in patterned wallpaper and fabrics. For a less formal, more countrified effect, colourwash the walls to produce a mottled look. The faded, sun-bleached corals also look great on exterior patio walls with terracotta floor tiles and plant holders to give a Mediterranean look.

The colour red is said to stimulate conversation and enhance the appetite. However, red walls could be overpowering in your home, so for your dining room a warm, coral pink is a good choice for making your guests feel at home.

▶ *Flushed with success*
An unconventional but highly successful combination of pink shades gives this large bathroom a warming glow. The mulberry pink paint used on the woodwork and the misty pink walls set off the unusual green bath and geometric-style flooring.

COOL PINKS

Cool pinks contain varying amounts of blue, a cold colour, in their make-up. This is why they are classed as cool, although all pinks add a certain degree of warmth to a colour scheme. The cool pinks include bright, shocking pinks, such as fuchsia and cyclamen, the clear shades of raspberry and mulberry, and the sugary pastel and mauvey pinks. Pale shades of pretty bluish pink are a popular choice for decorating bedrooms, while the boldest, vivid, shocking pinks unleash a fabulous sense of vibrant colour on a living or dining room.

A pastel-to-mid pink can be an incredibly seductive colour and works well in a bedroom. You can team it with plenty of glossy, white paintwork and floral fabrics in pink and white. In the evening, when the lights are low, the colour floods the room with a soft, romantic glow, flattering the palest complexion; and in daylight pastel pink is restful and relaxing.

There's certainly nothing safe or conservative about passionate shocking pinks. Such colours are not for the faint-hearted, but when handled with panache they can look really fabulous. Walls in this colour certainly create a dramatic effect and shocking pink fabrics and accessories add a touch of modern sophistication.

◪ A feminine approach

Soft pink is the perfect colour for decorating a pretty bedroom. This appealing blend of pale mauvey pinks and floral patterns creates a fresh, feminine look.

◣ Dramatic theme
Raspberry pink sofas add vibrant colour to an elegant, white living room. The pink and white theme is repeated in the curtain and cushion fabrics.

◣ A rosy glow
To avoid any hint of chill, this bathroom is decorated all over in carefully graduated tones of sugar-candy pink.

SHOCKING PINKS

Shocking pinks aren't always the easiest colours to use, but they team well with white or cream walls. There are some wonderful, exuberant fabrics around in brilliant pinks and greens. Try mixing fuchsia pink with apple green, warm gold or black, for example.

A bright raspberry pink sofa can also look fantastic in a living room with a blue-grey carpet and walls, or add a shocking pink bedspread to revitalize a neutral bedroom.

You won't need many ornaments with such a bold colour scheme – a few pieces of dark wooden furniture are all you need to make the perfect complement.

◣ Pink elephants
Pinks of all persuasions, whether from the mulberry or the coral side of the family, get on well jumbled up in an assortment of patterns on upholstery and accessories.

◢ In bloom
Vivid pink tulips wake up any room and add a cheerful finishing touch to a neutral colour scheme.

Pink with Other Colours

The colours that go well with pink depend mainly on how bold an effect you want to create. As always, the best schemes are created by carefully orchestrating warm and cool shades, adding punch with an accent colour or tonal contrast. Inspiration is to be found everywhere you look in nature – palest pink-tinted clouds against a clear blue sky, the golden stamens in the centre of a climbing rose or delicate pink apple blossom beside the first bright green shoots of spring.

The very paleness of some pinks makes them the ideal background for strong accent colours while a startling, bright, deep pink has a greater impact when teamed with other, equally definite colours. In modern settings, the bold, vivid pinks serve as emphatic accent colours against a severe black and white decor. Or they can soften and warm a gently elegant living room or bedroom in monochromatic greys or neutrals.

Floral freshness
Yellow and pink make perfect partners in this living room. As the ultimate in spring freshness, the floral fabrics and sponged walls would look good in a bedroom too.

Favourite partner
Pink has a natural affinity with green. It is a frequent pairing in nature and brings equal beauty to your interior decorating whether used as two plain colours together or in a multiplicity of patterns.

Opposites attract
Occasionally, pastel pink and baby blue escape from the nursery. In this bedroom, a warm, pale pink strikes up a happy partnership with a cool, pastel blue on the walls. The floral fabrics pick up on the same attractive colour theme.

PASTEL IMAGES

Seen in a fresh and adventurous light, pastels have an equally exciting part to play in creating state-of-the-art room schemes as they do in their more traditional role as a flattering backdrop for graceful living.

Strictly speaking, pastel shades are a base of pure white tinted with one of the primary colours, to give a paler, chalky version of the original pigments. In practice, the term is used more loosely to refer to any pale, whitened colour. Varying the amount of coloured pigment added to the white base gives a wide range of tones within the same colour. A tiny spot of orange added to a white base, for example, gives a warm white; when you add a touch more orange you reach a delicate bloom of peach. Strengthening the colour still further takes it through terracotta to a glowing apricot. However, the presence of white in its make-up prevents the intensity of the colour from becoming garish or overpowering.

Pale pastel shades are exceedingly familiar and widely used as decorating colours to set an unassuming background and soothing mood in elegant rooms. However, such delicate colours also more than repay a quick reappraisal in an energetic modern context. When you start using pastel colours in their more intense tones, or mixing paler shades with black, naturals and other stronger colours rather than regulation white, they emerge as vital contributors to the liveliest modern schemes.

Just because pastels are pale, they are by no means colourless. Here a chequerboard of soft, chalky colours on the floor and a quant painted table and screen illustrate the range and attraction of pastel shades.

CLASSICALLY SOFT AND GENTLE

The classic, pale chalky tones of shell pink, almond green, lilac, primrose and powder blue make quiet but refreshing backgrounds for busy living. Because pastels are undemanding colours, you can focus on just one for a single-colour scheme, using the same shade in various ways, mixing prints and plains in the same room. This is a useful device for a small space, as it allows light to diffuse gently round the room and blurs edges and hard lines, giving an illusion of space. Make sure you have plenty of textural interest or pattern contrast to give the look verve.

You can use the flat colour in emulsion for walls, either straight off the roller or in a broken colour effect such as ragging; or choose a paper in a cloudy pattern, shadow stripe or faint print. Then go to town with checks, florals and plains, all based on the same tone and lightened with touches of cream, white and grey. Carry the colour through on woodwork with a paler tone of the walls; or go for classic white to pick out architectural features and mouldings. For continuity, wooden furniture can take a pastel stain, limed and distressed or colourwashed effect.

Another traditional scheme is based on a pastel background wash for walls, harmonized by a couple of other shades cropping up as accents around the room – perhaps a light blue on the walls and carpet, highlighted with tiny pink rosebuds in a blue-ribboned chintz at the window, while the sofa is covered in a blue and green weave with pale pink cushions. Proportion is all-important; in this case a large quantity of blue, warmed with touches of pink and a hint of green works well.

As so often happens, it is not always the colours you use but the way in which you use them that makes all the difference to the final look. Soft pastel colours have a part to play in a modern context too. You can use all these gentle shades in close harmony with one another, in a simple, artless style which focuses on colour and texture rather than pattern.

◩ White gold

White woodwork is conventionally regarded as the perfect foil for the paleness of pastel walls and fabrics, helping to bring out their reduced colour. In this case, the upholstery and furniture are white as well to enhance the pale pink and gold colouring of the room still further.

◪ Blush centred

Even the subtlest of pastel shades add a crucial hint of colour to a room. The palest pink walls and the rosy sheer curtain suffuse this spacious room with a warm glow. Accent splashes of raspberry pink on the duvet highlight the bed.

◢ Contemporary colours

Gentle pastels can play an active role in a modern context too. Used in close proximity through a series of rooms like this, the effect is anything but bland. The tonal similarities promote a sense of continuity within varied colour schemes.

▶ Purely pastel

Traditionally, restrained pastel shades are used to set a restful mood. Here the merest trace of minty green on the walls and curtain fabric imbues the room with a cool freshness. Defined by white cornice and woodwork, the effect is airy and light.

MIXING PASTELS

One of the great strengths of the pastel range is the ease with which the different shades blend with, and tonally complement, one another. Such gregarious characteristics are put to good use in a multitude of subtle, unassuming patterns. Pastel designs are an excellent compromise when you want to introduce one or two patterned elements into a room without letting them rule the roost.

◤ *Reef encounter*
Rich pastel shades, in conjunction with neutral colours and natural materials create satisfying modern-looking rooms. Here, deep coral pink checks and accessories lift the room with a warming glow.

▶ Softly, softly pattern
Fabric and wallpaper designs worked out in pastel shades are often extremely subtle but nevertheless effective. Here the pale stripes on the wall and the reversed out floral pattern on the curtains are the perfect way to introduce faint, colour-coordinated patterns to an elegant room.

◀ Pastel panache
For a consistent scheme, fill a pastel-hued room with colour-related accessories in varying strengths of tone, from the tangy lemon yellow of the teacups to the pale misty blue of the vase.

▶ Subtle strength
The designs on this coordinated floral wallpaper and the extra wide border take full advantage of a range of strong pastel colours. Adding white to pure colour imparts a hint of softness that gives it a feminine quality without being pallid. In a young girl's bedroom, the brightness of more intense pastels are the perfect substitute for a bowl-you-over blast of primary colours.

IN OTHER COLOUR SCHEMES

Pastel colours are also effortlessly compatible with other colour stories. You can take a roomful of neutral tones, set out with natural surfaces like stone, terracotta, wood and linen, and drop in practically any pastel for a lift of fresh, light colour. You could use two or three rose-coloured lamp-shades to add a warm glow on winter evenings, or work a smattering of embroidery in the delicate green of just-burst-out-of-the-bud leaves on plain linen curtains for a breath of spring freshness.

In a business-like kitchen with streamlined wooden surfaces, it only takes a hint of dainty colour to add an individual touch of character. A softly pleated blind in faint shades of blue and primrose is unobtrusive and restful. To go with the rich glow of traditional mahogany or teak, slightly stronger pastels make a perfect foil, echoing the deep tones of the wood without challenging them.

You can also partner the classic combination of black and white with the softer tones of pastels. A stark, monochromatic scheme set against sugar pink or pistachio green walls takes on a playful air – great for a teenager's bedroom or a hallway. The magic works the other way round as well. A few high-tech spiky black lamps or a matt black dado rail significantly pep up all-over pastels.

Pastels love bolder colours too; try a vibrant aquamarine below a dado with a strong lavender above. When you are feeling utterly daring, you can set a bowl of scarlet roses clashing against a pink wall to liven up a bedside table.

RELATIVE STRENGTH

With perhaps more than a nod or two in the direction of the sun-drenched shores of the Mediterranean, California and Mexico, a whole new crop of lively, sunny pastels are now appearing on the paint colour charts. These colours still have a flat, chalky look but at the same time are more saturated with colour than the traditional pastels. These are the sort of colours that sing out in bright sunshine but even on a grey day can give a cheerful buzz to remind you of Greek taverna doorways or Californian sundecks.

Aquamarine blue, sugar-mouse pink and a warm banana yellow are fun shades you can use freely in broad sweeps of colour. They look at their best applied flat in two or three coats on a wall for depth of colour.

Strong pastels look good jostling side by side on the same article. For a powerful effect you can try painting each drawer of a chest of drawers in a different punchy pastel, or using three different plain cottons on the arms, back and seat of a squashy sofa. The Mexican custom of painting a broad, sketchy contrast band around doors and windows is another way of introducing an extra colour to a scheme.

☑ Good as gold

Strong pastels retain a slightly powdery quality combined with a depth of colour. Whitening the yellow of the walls and upholstery softens a powerful golden colour while preserving all its richness.

▶ Pastels bite back

On the evidence of this room, it would be hard for anyone to argue that pastels lack punch. Vibrant lime green walls are ideal for a minimalist setting, as they require little by way of accessories for impact.

☑ Natural setting

Potent pastels, such as this dense blue, are ideal for introducing a strong but not brash colour into a scheme based on natural materials like stripped pine and stone-effect surfaces.

NEUTRAL SCHEMES

You can put the quiet tones, subtle hues and smudgy contrasts of flexible neutral shades to good use in designing rooms that reflect your lifestyle rather than dictate it.

Often thought of as the colours without colour, the range of neutrals is vast. Strictly speaking, they span from black to white through all the greys, yet are also taken to include shades of cream, beige and brown, such as taupe, ecru, fawn and stone, and off-whites. Such neutral shades are infinitely versatile, forming the basis of many restful interior schemes, from restrained soft modern to high-powered glamour.

Many people shy away from a purely neutral scheme for fear it may be dull or austere. Current trends in interior design show nothing could be further from the truth. A fresh confidence and interest abounds in the unadorned good looks of neutral finishes. As well as being quite capable of holding centre stage in their own right, neutrals play an important part as an unassuming background for bolder accent colours.

The successful execution of a neutral scheme probably involves more initial thought and planning than a layout where colours reign supreme. You need to ensure that every element, from paint and fabric to ornaments and trims, pulls its weight. But once the scheme is established, it is very easy to live with, and leaves you free to insert further items without fear of colour conflict.

Cool, fresh white and cream fabrics and paint create a harmonious, restful setting. Natural wood and fibre matting supply all the back-up the neutral colour scheme needs, while shafts of sunlight create patches of significant brightness.

PURE WHITE

White is the absolutely colourless neutral. But for all its neutrality, you should not expect white to play a totally passive part in a scheme. As paint it can dazzle with its brightness on walls and woodwork, while as sheer fabric it forms a misty screen in front of windows and over beds.

Completely white schemes are the accepted, hygienic norm in a kitchen or bathroom. White walls refresh a living or dining room and a bedroom, too, reflecting the maximum amount of light during the day, even in a shadowy room. Indirect artifical lighting softens any tendency to harshness in the evening.

SUBTLE GREYS

There are greys from every part of the colour wheel; warm greys with hints of pink or heather in them, cool blue-greys or fascinating sludgy greeny greys that defy description by changing colour throughout the day. In all its hundreds of variations, grey is a delight to use, either as a foil to black and/or white, or blending easily with other soft and subtle colours.

If black and white is too blunt a contrast for your taste, setting different shades of grey off against white is an elegant compromise. For a cool, romantic bedroom, for instance, white walls decorated with a grey stencilled border, grey damask upholstery and gleaming grey silk curtains held back with ropes of pearls complement a bed dressed in snowy white cotton.

▶ *Monochromatic fashion*
An underplayed black and white layout has to be the height of living room chic. Delightful little touches, like the black piping on the sofas and the striped cushion covers, add all the detailing required.

BLACK AND WHITE

Monochrome schemes based on the extremes of black and white are really most dramatic. This is an old yet always up-to-the-minute decorating device, exploiting the attraction of opposites. Black is dark and receding while white is light and advancing, so they provide a powerful visual contrast. Combined with the clean-cut lines of contemporary furniture and high-tech lighting, black and white is a good choice for creating stylish, modern interiors.

◀ *Tranquil grey*
Grey and white together are the toned-down version of the black versus white contrast. Here, the lightest of grey walls sets a restful bedroom scene, with the crisp white bedlinen giving a bright lift and deeper grey picture mounts toning superbly.

▶ *Double cream*
Cream walls, a white bedspread and pale wood sounds like a formula for blandness. But in practice the mellowness of the paintwork, the texture in the quilt and the honey-coloured wooden dressing table create an extremely attractive country bedroom.

CREAMS AND BEIGES

Creamy colours – the slightly yellowed whites – are the mellow version of pure white. They are generally substituted for white in country and traditional-style decor, to create elegant, restful rooms. Cream is also a good colour for suggesting a slightly aged appearance.

For many years beige has been the ultimate safe choice for decorating – the colour scheme you choose for want of any other particular preference, or to provide a universal, all-things-to-all-colours sort of background. There are many shades of beige, from the creamy to the pinkish and slightly olive. By playing various colours, like a rich mushroom beige, on the wall off against paler versions on the ceiling and woodwork you can build up schemes of amazing complexity.

▶ *Neutrality*
Smart cream upholstery against a rich beige background is a recipe for creating an extremely elegant room.

NEUTRAL HARMONIES

The great charm of neutrals is their effortless compatability, so you are bound to find colour combinations that please you. Used in imaginative ways, these easy-going colours create satisfying and harmonious schemes of endless fascination. Next time you go to the beach, take a close look at an assortment of pebbles, stones and shells. You can use their blends of colours as a reference point for your decorating schemes, by studying the subtle interchange between dark slate grey, the sandy gold of flint pebbles and the veins of white marbling across chunks of granite.

Mixing grey and cream, as shown on the left for example, forges a refined combination that looks quietly understated yet smartly adult. You can start by sponging the walls in two shades of cream and painting the ceiling in ivory. Then you can introduce the grey – storm-cloud grey as an accent on door and window architraves, with the doors painted in a paler tone. The pale gold of sisal or jute natural flooring makes a textural contrast on the floor, with richly textured fabrics in clotted cream colours outlined and tied back with grey cord at the windows.

Far from being harsh, the contrast between the darkness of black and the paleness of cream is intriguing. Together, they are responsible for creating some very handsome room schemes with a thoroughly modern edge, like the one shown right.

◩ Suave and sophisticated

In this living room, various shades of grey and cream more than live up to their reputations for being the ultimate in understated style. The broken colour paint effects on the wall and furniture and the mixture of simple patterns suggest a Scandinavian style of decorating.

◩ On neutral territory

Regardless of room style, neutral colours always work out best in unfussy, streamlined layouts. The low-key blend of beige and cream in this soft modern living room is spontaneous and spacious. Notice how slightly darker neutral shades are strategically positioned around the room as accent features.

◄ **Modern lines**

A strong sense of design emphasizes the thrilling contrast between black and cream in this stylish bedroom. The bold, straight outlines of the four-poster bed, the picture frames and the border in the carpet form a defined structure for a host of abstract and geometric patterns.

IN FAVOUR OF NEUTRALS

There are many plus points when you opt for a scheme based on neutral tones.

❖ Muted, quiet tones like creams and greys provide a restful backdrop for today's hectic lifestyles.

❖ Neutrals are perfect for open-plan living areas where different parts of the room have various functions; coordinating the separate areas is far easier with soft tones that blend easily with each other and with other natural surfaces like wood or brick.

❖ For a hardworking family room, browny grey or charcoal colours which don't show dirt and wear and tear are a boon. Choose mottled, knubbly carpets and heavily textured upholstery fabrics, saving lighter tones for items that are easily cleaned, like cushion covers.

❖ Eliminating powerful colours casts the spotlight on the shape of the room itself and on the items in it. Play up any interesting architectural features with lighting, and go for contrasts by placing a spindly metal table in front of the plump curves of a sofa.

❖ Exciting textural details really come to the fore in a neutral scheme. Look out for surfaces with different textures – wallpaper with a raised, ribbed surface instead of a printed stripe, natural stone or wood flooring, cane or bamboo furniture, and textiles with patterns in the weave.

❖ Accessorize neutral colour schemes with natural materials that rely on their texture and shape for maximum effect – wicker baskets stacked with pine cones, a terracotta urn filled with seedheads or a panel of antique cotton lace over a bedhead all fit the bill.

▲ **Perfect harmony**

A striking room like this puts pay once and for all to any suggestion that neutral schemes are boring. Mid and charcoal-tones of grey look wonderful with pale beige walls.

NEARLY WHITES

As anyone who has tried to match white with white can testify, even this most neutral of neutrals can have a tinge of colour in it, which does not become evident until contrasted with another, purer white. Whites with the merest suspicion of another colour are most popular and widely used as neutrals, even though they are more accurately described as the palest of pastels.

You can buy ready-mixed, tinted white paints with a hint of colour, such as apricot, rose, midnight or apple, that takes the hard edge off a brilliant white. The tint tilts the room towards a colour theme, without committing you to a definite scheme. Use tinted whites to create light, airy rooms, with a warm touch of apricot or a romantic hint of pink, for example.

◀ *Country scene*
Neutrals and naturals are often treated as one and the same thing. Hence a coarse linen cover for the sofa in ecru – a stone shade of beige – set against a pale blue-grey wall, looks at home in a country setting.

▲ *Clotted cream*
A yellowy shade of cream cladding looks like the top of the milk above the white-tiled worktop in a country pantry.

◣ *A mere blush*
A delicate pale apricot on the walls is the perfect warming foil for cool, dove grey upholstery and a marble fireplace.

CONTRASTING COLOURS

*Expect some memorable, eye-catching results when you
set contrasting colours from opposite sides of the colour wheel
against each other in your decorating schemes.*

Colours are an exhilarating aspect of life, especially when two contrasting colours are used side by side in home decorating. The visual repartee between a bunch of rich purple irises and a yellow wall behind, for instance, is a joy to behold.

Many people shrink from including strong, out-of-the-ordinary colour schemes in their homes for fear of getting them wrong. Using tried and tested harmonies – blues with green, yellows and oranges – naturals or very muted or pale shades seems a much safer solution than experimenting with unexpected combinations of colours. Yet being a bit more daring in your choice of colours brings its own rewards.

Colours which contrast most strongly are those which face each other across the colour wheel. They are known as complementary colours, where each has within it the part of the spectrum lacking in the other, so that when put together they create a satisfying balance.

In their purest forms some pairs are easier on the eye than others; a brilliant scarlet and grass green are so close in tone that they appear to jump about when placed together. Yellow and purple, while direct opposites, are often different in tone – purple is darker than yellow so there is a natural balance.

While there are a number of simple rules to bear in mind when using contrasting colours, let your own instinctive sense of the joy of colour be your main guide. Just as in anything else, nobody knows what's right for you as well as you do yourself.

Contrast schemes lose none of their impact when worked out in slightly muted tones. The classic red and green contrast pairing is given a sophisticated twist in this living room by using coral pink with a golden green.

SOFTENED CONTRASTS

Contrasting colours don't have to be as intimidating as their reputation for being shocking and awkward to work with implies. Many popular colour schemes, fabric designs and coordinated ranges are actually based on a pair of complementary shades. Yet the contrast aspect of the pairings goes largely unrecognized because the colours are cleverly toned down pale or muted shades. The result is still interesting, but more restful on the eye than a strident contrast.

Rather than going for the colours in their pure form, slide round the colour wheel a little, picking a shade of blue with a touch of green in it to go with a coral-tinged orange. The colours are still rich in contrast, but not as powerfully so as the direct opposites, pure blue and orange.

Another way of achieving a similar subtlety is to move up and down the tonal scale of the two colours concerned, adding white to give a more pastel effect or black to muddy them a bit. The blue and orange bedroom illustrated on the next page demonstrates this clearly, with its floral print featuring a deep blue and apricot, repeated in the coordinated stripe and echoed again in the gentle peach of the bedspread. The colours have a rich, mutually enhancing glow but because the tones are softened to blue-green or navy and lighter peach and apricot there's no stark contrast.

Pink and green is a popular, tried and tested formula which appears in many guises, but is once again based on a pair of complementary colours – the clash of red and green. By softening the red with white to make pink, and adding a little blue to the green to give a forest green, you get a classic combination to experiment with – one with which you can achieve glorious results.

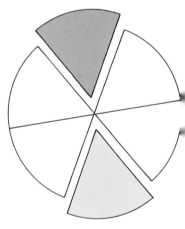

◄ *Yellow and purple*
A clever tactic for handling contrasting colours is to use them with a range of the harmonious colours around them on the colour wheel. Here, a variety of blues and greens forms a link between the yellow and mauve in a restful colour scheme.

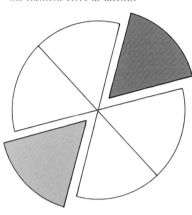

◀ *Pink and green*
This elegant living room exploits many shades of pink and green extremely successfully. Softened shades appear in intricate patterns in the curtains and upholstery while more intense shades on the cushions serve as accents.

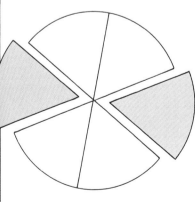

◀ *Blue and orange*
One way of making contrasting colours acceptable in home decorating is to use pastel and muted tones of a complementary pair. Here, modifying blue to navy and aqua, and lightening orange to apricot and peach, is remarkably soothing.

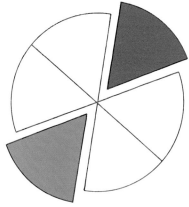

▲ Red and green

Tartans have mastered the art of balancing contrasting colours to perfection. In this dramatic living room, the strong dark green of the tartan fabrics, picked up in the paintwork, is the dominant theme. Yet the relatively small amounts of cheerful red featuring in thin bands in the tartan and the fringe shine out brightly, giving the whole potentially dour scene a great fillip.

▲ Blue and orange

If true blue sparked off with orange whets your appetite for a daring colour layout, then you might try giving the partnership a sympathetic background of colours against which to excel.

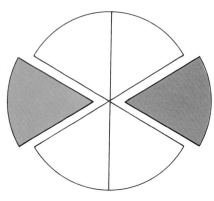

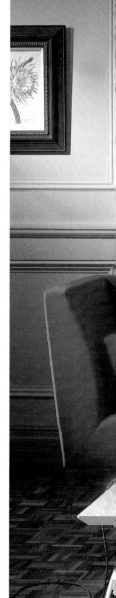

BOLD CONTRASTS

When you want colour schemes with a bit of snap and sparkle, then bold, bright complementary colours are the ones to use. If you have only ever lived with muted, pastel or neutral colours before, these vibrant colours may come as a shock to the eye at first. But if you break yourself in gently, courage is rewarded with a strongly individual scheme that is a hallmark of today's interiors.

When you want a medley of strong colours but are stuck for inspiration, you can always fall back on the old trick of using a striking patterned fabric or wallpaper as a reference. In addition to providing pointers as to which colours work well together, they also give clues about the best proportions in which to use them in your scheme.

The principle of proportion is all-important when dealing with powerful contrasting colours. Each colour influences the perception of the colour placed next to it. If two strong colours are seen in equal quantities the eye veers from one to the other, setting up uncomfortable vibrations, especially when they are strictly complementary pairs. This is because each complementary colour easily becomes its partners shadow, causing visual confusion. You can see it for yourself if you stare at a bright green object for 15 seconds and then close your eyes, a complementary magenta coloured after-image develops. In order to defuse the tension between the two colours, you must vary the quantity of each colour used.

When you decorate with contrasting colours, you are also playing a warm colour off against a cool one. When dealing with bold contrasts, it works best to use the receding cool colour over larger areas as a background for smaller accent touches of the advancing warmer colour. Covering a sofa in green and dressing it with pink cushions makes the most of a perfect partnership. The picture of the blue walls with a flash of bright orange flowers on the previous page illustrates the same point equally well.

☑ *Yellow and purple*
In this lively colour scheme, the yellow walls, purple chair, fiery red upholstery and lime green cushions all echo tones in the curtains' vigorous pattern. The colours play on their complementary and harmonious relationships.

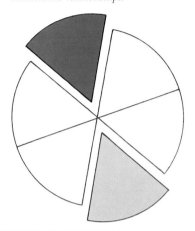

LIVELY CONTRASTS

Once you have shaken your mind free of colour clichés and safe harmonies, you can really start to enjoy scheming with colours. Opportunities for bending the rules arise all the time.

In the slightly unorthodox bedroom decorations below, for example, the warmer tones predominate, with several shades of red and pink on the walls, fabric and accessories. Using a relatively small amount of a single shade of bright green sets the whole scene buzzing.

It is this imbalance between the proportions of red, pink and their complementary colour, green, that makes the colour scheme successful. Not only do the areas of green on the bed-linen and wall establish a number of singing colour contrasts with the pinks and reds, but they also become the threads that draw the overall decor together.

◤ *Continuity factor*

A flash of totally unexpected colour, such as the vivid green band sparkling against the sugar pink wall, is all it takes to unite the decorations with the soft furnishings.

▶ *Surprise tactics*

A vase of informally arranged pink flowers and green leaves is one of those freewheeling elements of contrast that can slot in wherever and whenever the whim takes you.

The Importance of Tone

*If you can't put your finger on what is missing from a room scheme –
when it still looks rather bland or too busy, even after you've given a lot of
thought to the colour scheming – it's often the tonal mix that is wrong.*

The serenity of this colour scheme suggests a tonal harmony between the three pastel shades of pink, grey and cream paint, which the all-over greyness of the black and white print below confirms. Note how the wooden floor, furniture and frames introduce a deeper tone that prevents the scheme from looking bland.

Basically tone describes the lightness and darkness of a colour. If a colour is mixed with grey the subtler colour produced is referred to as a tone of the original. For example, rose is a particular tone of red, terracotta of orange, old gold of yellow, sage of green, Wedgwood of blue or dusky mauve of violet.

Technically the tone of a colour can be affected by two factors: its intensity – or brightness and strength – depending on the proportion of colour in the mix, and value, relating to the amounts of black and white it contains. Completely different colours can share the same tone because they have the same intensity and value.

To bring depth and light to a room scheme, it's important to end up with a tonal balance between all the colours used. If you decorate in only pale pastels, the outcome will be rather anaemic and wishy-washy; using only mid-tones, the effect runs the risk of being bland; when just deep tones are used, the room may be dull and gloomy. Distributing a range of tones throughout the room sparks a more vibrant and original look.

Once you can recognize various tonal intensities and values, and understand how to combine them appropriately, you will be able to create room schemes that buzz with interest as well as being pleasingly balanced.

Tonal Scheming

The easiest way to appreciate the benefit of tonal variety is to see it at work in a one colour scheme, where there are no other colours to confuse the issue. In this situation, a sensitive use of tones is particularly important to create a layout that is full of subtle changes in depth and lightness.

Creating colour schemes by combining different tonal versions of the same colour is the easiest of all design feats to pull off successfully. Lighter and darker tones of a single colour are naturally harmonious and pleasing to the eye, and there are hundreds of tints and shades to choose from to pep up the decorations in a room.

Be sure to include a range of tones that traces a gentle transition from the very pale to the extremely intense. Avoid leaps from one end of the tonal scale to the other that jar in a fluent layout. It's practical to use a mid-tone on the floor as a carpet, a paler version on the walls and the lightest one on the ceiling. Darker tones can be added in upholstery and accessories to anchor the scheme and provide focal interest.

With thought and planning, tonal similarities can be used to merge less desirable features into the background; extremes of tone can equally well draw attention to attractive details. When a fireplace is painted in precisely the same tone as the surrounding wall, for instance, its focal impact is less than if it is painted in a much paler or darker contrasting tone.

INCIDENTAL TONES

Daylight plays the most amazing tricks on a colour, creating highlights or areas of lighter tone, and casting shadows to form regions of darker ones. Such variability livens up the most relentless of monochromatic schemes. You can mimic the intriguing effects of natural light, and eliminate the vagaries of sunshine, by painting different parts of the room in varying tones.

When gauging the tonal scope of your scheme, take into account any dramatic areas of permanent shadow in pleats of fabric, or in the shadow cast by a wardrobe. These darken the tone of any colour, adding an extra dimension to the tonal scale plus movement to the overall scheme.

Also consider the contribution of any woodwork on doors, floors or furniture in assembling your scheme. Often these elements provide a crucial continuity and contrast over the entire room.

HOW TO TEST FOR TONE

To use tone successfully, you need to be able to distinguish between various tones of the same colour and similar tones in different colours. It's often hard to interpret the tonal relationship of colours when looking at a colour photograph. But in a black and white image, where colours are converted into shades of grey, it's more obvious. If you have access to a photocopier, you can get an instant black and white copy of fabric, wallpaper or paint swatches to help you see the tonal contribution of each colour.

To show up the differences in tonal values more clearly, a black and white print accompanies each colour picture in this feature. Compare the two images to familiarize yourself with the relative tonal quality of each area of colour and pattern.

PAINT CHARTS

You can see a broad range of tonal intensities and values demonstrated on the colour charts issued by the major paint manufacturers. The sample paint strips provide a shorthand way of instantly identifying and reproducing a specific tone. On each sheet the colours are graded according to the proportions of pure pigments mixed into a known quantity of blackness. By comparing codings between sheets you can match different colours that share the same tone.

To get a good range of tones of the same colour or between colours into your scheme you need to pick from various levels on the colour strips. Using the bathroom on the left as an example, the palest green from the paint strip (below right) appears on the walls, and deeper tones from further down the same strip, and a tonally related strip in blue, are used for coordinated towels and accessories.

Gentle transitions
The green and blue towels are clearly different colours, but show up as similar mid tones in black and white. The darker basket and chair, and white bath, add tonal variety.

Natural tones
Clever tonal scheming exploits the full scope of brown, from pale cream upholstery, through the natural timber of the mirror frame and floor to the dark tapes on the blind.

67

Tone & Colour

At first glance, it's natural to credit the individual colours used in a multi-colourful scheme for its success or failure. But when you look closer or longer, you can see that while some colour combinations work brilliantly well together, other mixtures of similar colours fall flat, simply because of a lack of tonal variation.

It's just as important to include a range of tones across all the colours in a scheme as it is to vary the tones in a single coloured scheme. You may have used a creative combination of blue, red and green, but if they are all of the same tone, the effect will still be flat. For a much livelier outcome, aim to involve a range of light, mid and dark tones – a pale green with a mid blue and dark red, for example, looks far more interesting.

When learning to assess the tonal range of a variety of colours, fabric designs provide a compact way of seeing a mixture of tones in different colours working well together. Pick a well-defined pattern that contains several colours. In many, you'll find that the two or three main colours are tonally very similar. The extremities of the range – the very light and the very dark tones – are often used sparingly as outlines and accents. Use black and white photocopies to confirm or correct your first impressions of the tonal arrangement.

You can follow a similar approach through in designing a whole room, distributing the deeper and paler tones to emphasize and outline specific features. Most skirting boards, architraves and window frames, for example, are either painted in a much darker or lighter colour to define the margins of the room.

Bridging tone

The black and white print above reveals that the striking bright orange of the chair covers is pitched at just the right mid tone to span the extremes of the black and cream decor.

Tonally correct

This elegant living room is both well colour coordinated and tonally correct. The bright yellow curtains and green cushion provide vital changes of tonal pace that wake up the whole scheme.

Saving grace

A good balance of light, mid and darker tones saves this room full of colours and patterns from degenerating into a visual mess. Distributing a range of tones round the room carries the eye easily from one area to another.

It's all too easy to fall into the tonal trap. By playing ultra safe with exactly matched colours and tones, a room can end up looking tame, and lacking an essential punch that gives it character. Relatively minor adjustments to the tonal content of a room can make the world of difference to its individuality.

Tonal imbalance in a decorating scheme is quite easily redressed by broadening the range of tones used. These two different treatments of the same bedroom show how a few fresh touches can lift a well coordinated but very pastel room.

It's neither complicated nor expensive to swap pale sheets for darker ones, sponge the wall in a deeper shade of pink, or add a rug and picture mounts in stronger tones to give the scheme impact. Take your colour cues from an item which is already part of the scene – in this case the pattern on the bedlinen.

COLOUR FLOW

When decorating separate rooms, it's important to think about how they fit into the rest of your home. Whole-house colour scheming takes an overall view, ensuring that colours flow from room to room.

Creating a harmonious and pleasing effect in decorating any room is a satisfying achievement. And while it's desirable for each room to have a distinctive character of its own, at the same time, it's important to think of the house in its entirety too. You want to avoid an impression of bittiness and establish a feeling of harmony as you move through the house. With some careful planning, by using colour to lead the eye on from room to room and a few clever designer tricks, it's possible to create a feeling of continuity and spaciousness throughout your home, regardless of its size.

Any part of the house where one room or space leads directly on from another benefits from a related view of planning. Living rooms, dining rooms and kitchens often have interconnecting doors or archways, or are merely different areas of the same room, and while they need a varied approach in practical terms, they should also complement one another. Likewise, en-suite bathrooms and dressing rooms leading off a bedroom should sit well with the main scheme.

The entrance hall and landing are also crucial areas of design distribution, with several doors opening off them. When visualizing their colour scheme it helps to leave all the doors leading to the adjoining rooms open. You can then see how the hallway and landing walls and architraves act as a frame for these rooms.

The impact of colour flow really registers in an open-plan situation. In this light, modern room, not only are the bright rainbow stripes on the rug echoed in the narrower, paler stripes on the chair covers beyond, but the use of identical blinds throughout adds a sense of uniformity as well.

CREATING CONTINUITY

You can employ all sorts of devices to set up a sense of design harmony in your home. Apart from straightforward colour links, patterns, furniture and accessories all serve their purpose in reinforcing a consistent decorating theme from room to room.

The simplest way to handle the different colours in the rooms leading off a hall or landing is to pick several shades of the same colour. In this way, they harmonize without appearing bland. Alternatively, you can choose a striking and flexible combination, like black and white, as the colour theme for your home, and mix it with rich, natural finishes in wood and wicker in an imaginative blend of textures and shapes – this allows you to vary the look in many ways without altering the colour story. Or you can choose a calming base colour like cream for the walls, and add various accent colours in different ways to vary the mood of the rooms.

UNIFYING FLOORING

You can achieve visual continuity and a feeling of spaciousness by using the same or similar colour floorings throughout your home. For instance, a honey or tan carpet in the hall and on the stairs works well with slightly darker floor tiles in the kitchen and a toning plain caramel carpet or stripped floorboards in the living and dining rooms.

You can add islands of colour on natural wooden floors in the form of rugs and dhurries to vary the look of each room. If you buy rugs in similar colours, they can also link various flooring areas round your home.

▶ *Go with the flow*
In this en-suite arrangement, the connection between the bedroom and the bathroom is taken very literally. The wall and floor treatments are identical, and similar dark wrought-iron style furnishings in both rooms reinforce the link.

◀ *A light link*
Looking through from this dining room into the living room next door reveals a subtle continuity between the two. The cool cream wallpaper with its delicate blue wreath motif is echoed by the plain cream walls in the adjoining room, while a soft blue recurs on the curtain fabrics in both rooms.

▶ *A sneak preview*
Even in an L-shaped room where there is a consistant yellow background, the rest of the colour scheme can change abruptly as you round the corner. A tiny foretaste of the adjoining colour scheme, such as the bright red and blue of the flowers and the lamp, serves to herald the explosion of colour to come.

A SEQUENCE OF PATTERNS

Coordinated patterns are another excellent way of creating intricate interchanges of colour between different areas. Many fabric and wallpaper ranges feature large and small motifs, like checks, in the same colourway, so you can play the theme back and forth, from sofa to kitchen walls and back to chair covers, without it becoming overpowering. In a similar way, hanging the same patterned wallpaper through the hall and up the stairway to the landing above creates a roomy feeling as it leads the eye upstairs. When colour scheming for adjoining rooms, you could then pick up different shades from the patterned paper, so that the rooms and hallway relate to each other through the print.

ARCHITECTURAL DETAILS

Architectural details in the form of dado and picture rails or skirting boards can also work as harmonizing visual threads, carrying colour along corridors, across landings and even up stairs to provide a bond between two storeys.

A lovely way of highlighting a multi-doored entrance hall in an older house is to strip and wax all the interior doors in the house, so that the initial flavour of the hall spreads throughout. Then pick a single subtle colour, like a soft grey or pale, powdery blue, that you can take through the whole house on architraves and skirting, to frame the waxed doors uniformly.

◤ *Patterned solidarity*

Coordinated ranges are a great aid to colour and pattern flow. Two distinct areas of this house are linked simply by using the same floral pattern on the wallpaper in the hallway as for the two cushion covers on a chair in the living room.

SHOCK TACTICS

Colour flow is far from being about creating dull uniformity throughout your home. Big bold contrasts can work just as well as subtle colour links, but they need careful planning for maximum effect. Looking through a series of rooms with strong, flat planes of contrasting colour resonating against each other is either a richly exhilarating or painfully uncomfortable experience. You need to think such a daring approach through by walking round from room to room, visualizing the points where the colours will converge. Painting the intervening woodwork in a single, neutral colour helps to create a dividing line where the colours meet.

◨ Bridging the divide
Pictures are strong attention grabbers, so they make ideal pointers to lead the eye through the house. While the flooring and the colour scheme change dramatically at the threshold to the dining room from the hallway, floral prints in similar frames on the walls preserve an essential sense of unity.

◩ Through and through
A direct approach to designing your home often produces the most effective results. Decorating the whole house in variations on a favourite colour scheme, like a sandy beige and grey, inevitably gives rise to a sense of overall harmony.

◨ In outline
White-painted doors, architraves and skirting boards draw a common thread between the various rooms leading off this landing. To reinforce a sense of belonging, the deep peach colour used on the walls is repeated as a dotted pattern on the blue wallpaper in the room beyond.

PATTERN AND MOOD

You can set any mood you like in your home by choosing the right patterns – be they bright checks or stripes for a lively up-to-date feel or florals and textured damasks for a traditional town house look.

Most patterns have a clear identity. Not only do their design motifs place them into a specific category – either as a floral, check or stripe and so on – but also closely ally them to a particular period or style of decorating. So, while a fine stripe is associated with the graceful elegance of a Regency living room, a jazzy stripe has a more here-and-now feel about it. Some familiar patterns, notably tartans, are seen to have a marked regional bias. You can turn these relationships to your advantage in your decorating by using patterns that reinforce the scene

A well-judged blend of patterns – discreet stripes, a large floral and bold checks – establishes a restful ambience for a small living room.

TEXTURED

In textured designs, a muted pattern is derived from subtle changes in shade, texture or weave, rather than worked out in a variety of colours. This device is widely used on wallpaper, fabric, tiles and carpets to add interest and detail to the surface.

Many fabrics, like damasks for example, have intricate patterns which rely on a reversal of the weave in different areas. The resulting design catches the light in different ways, giving a beautiful subtle effect without strident colour contrasts. Some wallpapers feature a satiny stripe on a matt ground; others, like the old fashioned relief and flock papers, have a raised pattern.

All these surfaces offer opportunities to add definition and life to a scheme without adding extra colour. Traditionally, the intriguing subtlety of such textured patterns has played an important part in elegant, restrained situations such as a town house living room. Today they are also ideal for creating interest in the latest neutral schemes, where colours are kept to a minimum for a cool, natural look.

ABSTRACT

Abstract patterns tend to be much freer and less rigid than more formal or naturalistic designs, giving an irregular, slightly quirky look to textiles and papers. Some are based on geometric shapes dispersed haphazardly across the background. Others feature free brushstrokes and random splashes of colour as part of the design.

New designs on fabrics, wallcoverings and accessories are constantly evolving to reflect contemporary design trends, take advantage of the latest printing techniques or re-interpret traditional motifs in a modern idiom. Many are executed in vibrant colours which gives them a light-hearted, almost rebellious image. Combined with black and white, or blocks of strong plain colours, and metal furniture they make an up-to-the-minute design statement.

FLORALS

The appeal of flowers is universal. Through the centuries floral motifs have been interpreted and reworked many times in hundreds of different ways.

Small floral designs have pretty, delicately coloured blooms repeated every few centimetres or so. They are perfect for capturing a cottagey look in a kitchen or bringing a fresh innocence to a bedroom layout.

Larger floral patterns can have a glorious, summer-garden-in-full-bloom impact on a room. But watch out for really big pattern repeats; it would be a shame to have to chop a full-blown rose in half along the top or bottom of a wall – better to choose a smaller pattern.

These designs may be overpowering in large quantities, but smaller amounts can be worked in carefully with other small floral, stripes, checks and plains. This policy is widely adopted in many coordinated ranges. Halls, bedrooms, large sitting rooms and dining rooms are all suitable locations for bold treatments.

In the modern, stylized versions, impressions of flowers rather than realistic representations are drawn into strong patterns – circular motifs, for example, or continuous, undulating lines. There is a huge variety of interpretations; many of the designs, like lotus flowers and agapanthus used in brocades, date back to Greek and Roman times. They can be used to add style and dignity to a traditional scheme, or blend in well with a more contemporary look.

The popularity of floral motifs is such that they are often found combined with other patterns in a single design – stripes interspersed with rows of rosebuds, for instance, or interwoven with swags of twisted ribbon.

STRIPES

With their adjacent bands of different colours or tones, stripes are among the most versatile of patterns. There is a stripe to suit all situations and decorating ambitions and, when used with panache, stripes can play the cleverest of visual tricks, making low ceilings look higher and narrow hallways broader.

Discreet self-patterns are the ones to turn to when you want a subtle, textured effect coupled with the orderliness of straight stripes. Perfectly straight stripes, whether self-coloured or in sharp contrasts, have a classic, calm feel that brings a sense of formality to a room's layout. They provide a structured background against which to arrange the rest of your furnishings.

When the need arises, bolder, multicoloured stripes make a forceful impression. Used with a confident hand, they form the basis for cheerful and lively schemes which are particularly appropriate for children's rooms. For a more controlled option, the simplest of stripes – bands of one colour on a white or cream background – are perfectly suited to modern apartment style rooms, and make a fresh backdrop for informal furniture styles.

CHECKS

Always fresh and outstanding, woven checked designs are hugely popular, versatile and practical. As natural mixers, they are frequently blended in with other, more flamboyant designs in coordinating ranges.

Gingham, Madras, dogtooth and windowpane checks all have a no-nonsense functional feel and disguise dirt and stains well. Such checked cottons have graduated from use as summer slip covers for protecting furniture in eighteenth century houses to play a prominent role in today's interiors. Light, spartan Scandanavian interiors characteristically feature colourful checked cotton on chairs and at windows. On walls, an unobtrusive check can help to unify a motley scheme by fixing individual pieces in a frame.

As with any design, the colours of the checks have a significant bearing on the impression they create. Generally, strong, vivid colours are equated with a bold, jubilant modern approach, while softer, more muted shades translate more satisfactorily into traditional or country schemes.

TARTANS

Originally a woollen clothing textile, these patterns were the uniforms by which different Celtic clans recognized each other. Large blocks of colour are broken up by narrow lines of contrasting tones, often in strong combinations like deep greens, red and black. Now produced on cotton, silky taffeta, wallpaper, bedlinen and even cups and saucers, these patterns are very effective in the home, either mixed together or with other designs. Good for atmosphere in a study or a boy's bedroom, they can also create a cosy, warm traditional dining room, highlighted with polished wood and pewter.

ETHNIC

The glorious colours and vigorous designs of exotic, faraway places bring an exuberant flavour to an interior. The sources of inspiration are varied and colourful – like their places of origin. Textile houses draw from tie-dye cottons and vibrant weaves of Africa, batik from Indonesia, ikat weaves from Japan or the kelim rugs of the Middle East, so it's possible to find fabrics by the metre that capture closely the essence of the original cloth.

For an interesting mix, include lengths of authentic fabrics in a scheme. Indian dhurries, batik bedspreads or ikat weaves all blend well with the elements of a traditional or modern scheme and alongside other patterns.

PROVENÇAL AND PAISLEY

Both Provençal and Paisley patterns have developed over the centuries from patterns on Indian textiles. Their common origin is apparent from the shared teardrop or cone motif.

Provençal colours reflect the brilliant countryside of the South of France – sunshine yellow, rich earthy red and deep blue. The busy designs with their small, repeated motifs work very well closely intermingled with each other. Try using one small sprig repeated in reverse colourways on curtains, a bedspread, tablecloth or place mats. Set this medley of prints against lots of rich dark wood and terracotta flooring for an open-air feel in a conservatory or garden room.

Paisleys are named after the Scottish town which became famous for weaving and printing imitation Kashmiri shawls in the eighteenth century. The curled teardrop motif is repeated over the design to give a dense swirling pattern. Each motif has a fine infill of flowers, leaves or birds. Colours were originally rich and exotic, but now Paisleys are often worked in soft mauves and blue to echo the Highland glens. Combine it with tartan for a Scottish feel, or give a dining room drama with deep red walls and glowing Paisley curtains.

CHECKS

Checked patterns are once again at the forefront of home design, appearing on fabrics, wallcoverings and numerous accessories. Their crisscrossed bands of colour convey a simple freshness and crispness wherever they are used.

Once reserved for kitchen curtains or the nursery tablecloth, checks are today's hot fashion favourite for every part of the home. In their simplest woven form, the designs consist of intersecting bands of different colours running at right angles across each other, forming alternating blocks of colour. These bands can vary from a narrow pinstripe to a wide swathe of colour, or a mixture of the two. As each set of threads crosses other colours, new colour blends emerge, creating a wonderful variety of effects.

Many of the great classic patterns – especially in textiles – come from the check stable: gingham, tartan, plaid, dogtooth tweed, Prince of Wales checks and Madras cottons, bursting with eastern colour.

When the basic check pattern is printed rather than woven, there is scope for combining checks with flowers, leaves, spots and dots, zigzags or twirls in more elaborate designs. They appear on fabrics, wallcoverings, carpets and ceramics for you to enjoy in your home.

Checks are one of the simplest yet most variable of pattern themes, ranging from simple squared designs to richly coloured, intricately woven grids.

81

FOURSQUARE AND FUNCTIONAL

The straightforward chequerboard styles of check have a brisk, no-nonsense feel. In its hardworking, stain-disguising fashion, gingham brings a rustic simplicity to a plainly decorated room or a cheerful, unpretentious touch to the grandest of settings – an age-old trick that still works today. Draping an elaborate four poster bed with blue and beige checked linen has a cool, understated elegance, and is a clever way of integrating period furniture into a modern room scape.

Tiny or fine checked patterns are useful if you want a pattern but not an obvious design. Seen from afar, the bands of colour blend into each other. When choosing these mini-checks, it's a good idea to view them from a distance as well as close to; you may find that the blue and red check you wanted for covering a sofa blurs into a purplish tinge from the other side of the room.

Bigger checks can have a powerful but controlled effect on a scheme. For example, floor length curtains in a huge black and white check form the basis for a bold modern scheme using up-to-the-minute colours, with lime green on the walls

and a stack of shocking pink cushions on the sofa.

A large area of checked or squared pattern can serve as unifying background for a wide mix of objects. A simple graph paper style checked wallpaper in blue or snappy red on white will give a trendy but smart look to a functional kitchen, and works well with shiny laminated surfaces, high-tec steel and plain strong colours.

Softer, smudgy checked papers will disguise imperfect wall surfaces without imposing a rigorous pattern. Tartan covered walls give a wonderfully cosy but gutsy feel to a study or dining room.

Even floors glory in the check effect. Black and white tiles alternating across a hall floor conjure up a mansion like elegance, and increase the sense of space by pushing the walls outwards. Borrow the business like grid patterned carpet used in modern offices for duty in a soft modern living room.

For a more subtle parquet flooring effect, use two toning woodstains on alternate sanded floorboards, then repeat the stripes across the boards at right angles to give alternate blocks of slightly different woodtones.

◀ An open check
A minimalist version
of a checked design,
called windowpane
check, on the sofas
introduces a perfect
touch of unfussy
pattern to a soft
modern living room.

▽ Squared up
For the most chequered of all checks –
and a dramatic finish to a bathroom wall
– it's hard to beat black and white tiles
set out in chessboard fashion.

▲ Eye-checking
When they're big and bright enough, checks cut
quite a dash. There's certainly no ignoring the
bold checked pattern on
this duvet cover.

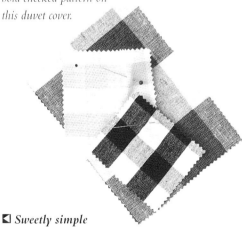

◀ Sweetly simple
A fresh mixture of two blue
and white checks on the walls and cot
drapes conveys just the right degree of
innocent charm in a young child's room.

◀ Bistro checks
Here a cheerful
red and white
gingham fabric is
working on
familiar territory
– hanging as café
style curtains at a
kitchen window.

START WITH A CHECK

Many a colourful check design can form the starting point for a lively decorating scheme. Use one fairly strong check for a sofa or in the curtains – say a blue, rust and gold Madras cotton. Then choose single colours for other elements in the room, picking out the golden yellow for the walls, rust for the carpet and a single easy chair in vibrant blue.

Different checked patterns are usually highly compatible. Many fabric companies produce the same checked design in a large and small scale; these will blend happily together in a room – use the smaller version of the curtain check for cushions, or perhaps use one to bind the other on a bedspread or tablecloth. Such a mixture of various sizes and colours of check creates a rather jolly, relaxed effect which is fun in a family living room, a kitchen or a child's bedroom or playroom.

Checks easily complement other designs too; their orderly crisscross motif means they don't hijack the design theme – unless they are particularly large or strident and consequently totally unmissable. Try teaming long curtains in a splashy gold, green and cream rose print with a straight pelmet or tiebands in a toning check of the same gold and green. Pick out the deep green in a braid or cord to edge the pelmet and tiebands.

Stripes and checks are made for each other, and often occur as partners in coordinated wallpaper and fabric ranges. Use a busy check up to the dado rail and a calmer stripe above. A swirly border pattern in between will break up the lines. Or bind the leading edge and base of cool striped curtains in a beige and white linen with a small toning check. Natural shades blend easily together – mixing patterns is a good way of sparking up the scheme.

▲ *Spic–and–span*
The regular crisscross of the checked upholstery maintains a seemly sense of order in a light, minimally furnished room.

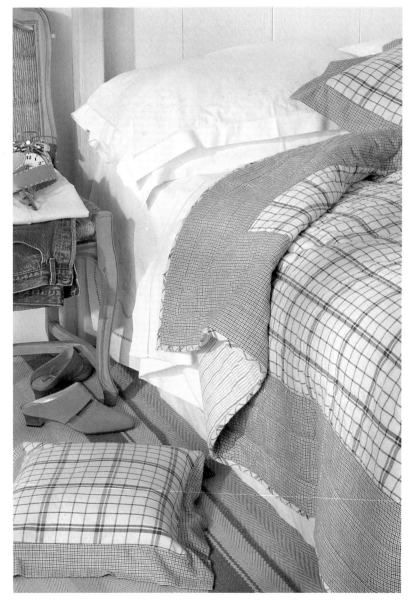

◀ *Universal appeal*
Graph paper checked bedlinen happily solves the dilemma of finding an acceptable pattern for a boy's or young couple's bedroom.

▶ *Easy-going*
Playing mix and match with different coloured check patterns in the cushion covers and curtains creates a comfortable, casual image for this modern living room.

▲ Background material

Checks provide the groundwork for further patterning in the liveliest of coordinated fabrics and wallcoverings. Here the floral checked fabric is clearly derived from the vivid checked wallpaper – as a result the two work perfectly together.

ACCESSORIES

There are many checked items around to liven up the domestic scene. Multicoloured cushions, kilt-like lampshades, even gaily checked cups and saucers are easy to find in major stores. For extra colourful effects, drape a bright plaid throw over a plain sofa, wake up your bedroom with a daringly bold check, or brighten a bathroom with one dazzling orange and blue checked towel.

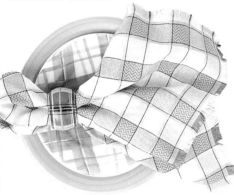

▲ Tableware
Cheer up the dining table with gaily checked china and napkins.

▷ Along these lines
A check paper folds neatly into a sharply pleated lampshade.

▲ All the difference
It only takes one cushion cover with a larger check to give the colour scheme in this window treatment an extra special buzz.

◁ Underfoot
These lino tiles make a trim and practical alternative to the traditional black and white chequerboard flooring.

▷ Headlines
Brightly checked pillowcases are a great way to liven up plain sheets.

STRIPES

Among the most disciplined of patterns, stripes can be cool and calming, bright and breezy, smart and chic – but never boring. They readily adapt to any decorating style and blend harmoniously with many other designs.

Nature loves stripes. You only have to think of the tabby cat or the tiger, the yellow and black hoops of a wasp or the monochromatic zebra to appreciate how effective alternating bands of different colours are at attracting attention or serving as camouflage.

Such purposeful ways with stripes can inspire adventurous decorating schemes as well. Whether the stripes are broad or fine, crisp or blurred, delicate or dramatic, simple or riotously complicated, they retain a typical sense of order and smart gaiety.

Stripes are easy mixers, happy to collaborate with each other or more elaborate floral, geometric and ethnic patterns in dazzling decorating schemes. To avoid a confusion of patterns, aim to maintain at least one clear link between the designs. Choose stripes in the same colours but different widths, for example, or stick to the same scale of stripe in varying colours. For a more casual effect, mix and match stripy patterns which look as though they have been freely hand painted rather than rigidly ruled.

Branching out from solo stripes, try balancing a boldly striped wallpaper against a coordinating floral fabric or paper. Luckily many coordinated collections of fabrics and wallcoverings include a stripe, plus a variation on the striped theme, to make your choice easier. It's then up to you whether you feature stripes as the main scene setters or as a regimented foil for more flamboyant or discreet patterns.

Left to their own devices, stripes of all colours and widths are quite capable of carrying off an entire design scheme – as the rainbow of striped fabrics in this cool bedroom confirms.

87

VISUAL TRICKS

One of the greatest advantages of stripes as a decorating tool is their visual craftiness. Used skilfully, they can cunningly distort the dimensions of a room or a feature in it.

A series of vertical lines running parallel to each other has the effect of lengthening and narrowing the object to which they are applied, so a low ceiling can be visually pushed higher by covering the walls with a striped wallpaper. Similarly a low window can be made to appear taller by curtaining it with a bold vertically striped fabric.

Most woven striped fabrics are vertically striped, with the different colours occurring in the warp or long vertical threads of the material. Some have very narrow stripes formed of only one or two threads, separated by wider areas of contrast colour; pin stripes, ticking and candy stripes are all familiar favourites. Others, like deckchair canvas, have wide regular bands of colour. Still others rely on a change of texture caused by a different weave or thread to create a subtle shadow stripe. These are useful for upholstery where a plainer fabric would show wear.

Some fabrics overlay a woven stripe with another pattern, in a sumptuous striped damask, for example, or alternate a plain band of colour with a contrasting band bedecked with flowers or leaves; a moiré effect is sometimes added for a glamorous gleam. Yet more variation is available with printed fabrics, either in simple regular stripes or contemporary splashy designs. Other prints have bands of differing patterns in subtle blends of colour, perhaps filling one stripe with a paisley pattern while another has a tiny check.

Side to side stripes
Horizontal stripes make surprisingly few appearances in home design. Yet they are useful for making an area look wider or shorter than it really is. This window wears its striped curtains like a casual poncho, to suit the spicy, stripy scenery.

Ever upwards
A vertical striped wallpaper above the dado exaggerates the height of this bathroom ceiling, but in a sunny yellow that prevents it looking too cavernous.

Soft lines
Striped upholstery is an excellent way of introducing a controlled amount of pattern and colour to a modern living room.

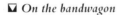

▶ Reversed out

Apart from being brazen and fun, stripes score highly for their elegant simplicity. Here, using the reversed colourways of a fine stripe in opposite directions for the curtains and on the stool has stylish consequences for the whole room. Note too how the radiator and the railings on the balcony reinforce the striped theme.

▼ On the bandwagon

An artful use of striped fabrics and wallcoverings can convey subtle effects. Almost incredibly, three different stripes and the bedstead are working together in this bedroom without making it look extraordinarily stripy. Only the zebra stripes on the cushion immediately claim the attention.

WAYS WITH STRIPES

Inexpensive ticking or candy striped cotton can be dressed up to look truly sophisticated by trimming it with a plain colour. Use black piping and buttons to trim a tab heading on black and white ticking curtains and loop them back with a huge black tassel. Even a simple but generous band of green border around a cool green candy striped cotton roman blind makes it look smartly tailored.

For an equally clever effect, reverse this look and bind a plain blind or square table-cloth with a wide striped border, setting the stripes at right angles to the edge. Match the mitres carefully at the corners so that the stripes form a well aligned chevron pattern. Add a tiny tassel or pompon to draw attention to the fine detail.

Aligning stripes against stripes so that they run at right angles to each other can be most eye-catching. In this way, an abundance of stripes can work successfully and interestingly with one another.

Pinchpleats or goblet pleats on striped curtains look much better if the pleats are worked out to coincide with the stripes. You will need to work this out before you finish the side seams so that you can make the necessary adjustments to the width.

DIAGONAL STRIPES

Cutting striped fabrics on the bias, as you would for piping, gives diagonal stripes which open up a whole new range of design possibilities. Use bias cut strips to cover a very thick piping cord or a roll of

◩ Paint strips

Improvised stripes, like the blue and white ones painted on this wall, are full of impact. Bands of equal width are masked off with low-tack tape on an all white wall, and every alternate strip is painted blue.

◪ Parallel rows

There are more ways of creating a striped pattern than with regular, straight bands of colour. In this case, twining sweet peas up the wallpaper in well spaced strips of blue and yellow gives a stripy impression with a floral twist.

wadding to edge curtains, bedspreads or loose covers. Jade green cushions edged with blue and green stripes stand out splendidly on a deep blue sofa, while a creamy bedspread edged with subtle grey, beige and cream stripes gains a sophisticated distinction.

With a touch of ingenuity you can create a clutch of eye-catching cushions quite inexpensively using scraps of striped fabric by dividing the front of the cushion into four and alternating the direction of the stripes. For another cushion, the fabric could be cut on the bias and then treated in the same way as four panels, so that the stripes create a diamond pattern. Or just use a striped border to create a prominent frame for a central floral panel.

INCIDENTAL STRIPES

Interesting results can be achieved when you aim to incorporate the stripes that crop up coincidentally in your overall room scheme – perhaps the shadows through the slats of a venetian blind, the bars of a brass bedstead or the self stripes of tongue-and-groove panelling.

▲ *A striped mural*
Sometimes the stripiness of a pattern is almost obscured by extra decoration. In this case, the blue and white bands on the wallpaper and fabric are attractively augmented by exotic eastern images.

◀ *All ways round*
To the delight of home decorators, stripes are incredibly adaptable. This sofa would look quite different if the same cushions were to be propped up with their stripes running parallel to, rather than counter to, the striped upholstery.

Stripes on Walls and Floors

A subtly striped wallpaper is the easiest way to add understated elegance to any room. Besides giving an illusion of height, the pattern acts as an undistracting background to the rest of the decorations and soft furnishings. Try fresh blue and white fine stripes to set off pine furniture in a country-style bedroom, with a muslin draped bed and flower strewn cotton curtains. Or opt for a neo-classical living room with a wide beige and grey stripe to set off architectural prints and finished with a Greek key design border.

Strong stripes on floors are best kept to small areas like rugs, otherwise they can dominate the room. But cotton dhurries in gay colours, or brightly banded runners for halls and staircases, are an inexpensive and effective way of adding colour and cheer to a scheme.

◀ **Temporary stripes**
During a stripy phase, curtains and a bathmat are an easy way to introduce the pattern of the moment without making drastic changes.

▼ **Wavy lines**
Fine multi-coloured curvy stripes make a jolly decoration that enhances the fluid lines of a shallow ceramic bowl.

Stripy Details

Small amounts of a striped pattern can be very effective because of the way they catch the eye. Contrasting bands of colour can be used to focus attention on an important feature: a wooden mirror frame striped with bands of alternating light and dark stains, or black and cream piping on a a plain cream sofa go a long way to livening up the whole scheme. A boldly striped roller or roman blind adds significant impact to a window. Try covering a motley collection of photograph frames in different but coordinating stripes to tone with the room. Or choose brightly striped mugs or plates to range along a shelf in a pristine white kitchen.

▲ **A classic case**
With stripes, there is no need to sacrifice elegance for practicality. A stripy papered dado will stay smart while taking a battering.

▶ **Colourful fun**
Let vibrantly striped fabrics inspire some equally colourful painted stripes on walls, shelves and storage containers.

DEFINING FLORALS

Floral patterns capture the vitality and colourfulness of fresh flowers and leaves in a myriad of different ways. Whatever your chosen room style, there is a floral design to enhance it.

The choice and distribution of appropriate patterns is an important aspect of decorating any room style. As far as floral patterns are concerned, certain room styles are obviously more dependent on a dominantly floral look than others to set their characteristic mood. A cottage without flowers, for instance, is as difficult to visualize as a Scottish-style interior devoid of tartan.

The flowery patterns on offer are generally divided into three main categories: full-blown large florals, all-purpose medium florals and dainty mini-prints or sprigs. Within each grouping, you find all sorts of representations of flowers, from the wholly realistic to the highly abstract, in terms of colour, form, background and spacing.

With so many floral patterns to choose from, deciding on which ones are best suited to your favoured room style may seem perplexing. In practice, however, as you think about the key points of each room style, you find that the most suitable florals virtually select themselves. A huge, splashy floral wallpaper looks wonderful in a town house dining room, for example, but totally out of place in a streamlined, contemporary setting.

Where and how you use florals is as important as which florals you choose. In keeping with the overall flavour of each look, an isolated flash of floral pattern on a blind is as significant in a soft modern bedroom or living room as the layering of multiple florals in a Victorian-style dining room.

The following pages show a selection of pictures, each one chosen because it epitomizes the most appropriate, mood-enhancing floral pattern for its particular room style. The accompanying fabric swatches suggest alternative versions of the right sort of floral pattern for each look. Use these pictures as a guide when you're choosing floral designs for your own home.

Sometimes the shock of using a traditional floral design in an unconventional situation can work wonders in bucking up the room and shedding a fresh light on the pattern.

AMERICAN COUNTRY

In keeping with its strong affliliations to the graceful, hand-made simplicity of the Shaker style, the American country floral is neat and orderly. Small, modestly coloured sprigs are often kept in line with a straightforward check or stripe. Mock stencil and patchwork effects with a folk-craft quality are also perfect. Floral designs of any sort are used quite sparingly, with plenty of natural woodwork and muted greens, blues and pinks of the Saker style.

❖ **Look for:** small, well-spaced floral motifs arranged tidily on dusky or cream coloured backgrounds.

COTTAGE

Flowery patterns are a key element in creating the intimate, friendly cottage mood. Floral motifs, reminiscent of country lanes and cottage gardens, are one of the best ways of evoking the country cottage look in a kitchen, bathroom or bedroom. The scale of the patterns is crucial - small rooms call for sprigged to medium-sized designs, often used together in a galaxy of florals. The most obvious quality of country-style small to medium florals is the prettiness of their carefully executed, realistic flowers.

❖ **Look for:** a mixture of well-spaced sprigs on pale pastel or cream backgrounds and lifelike, flower-strewn patterns in pretty, realistic colours.

APARTMENT

A daring blast of bright colours is the foundation of the budget-conscious apartment look. At first sight, it is not a style in which floral patterns are welcome, let alone play a starring role. The sharply geometric lines of the furniture and a vivid colourfulness generally carry the style. Any floral pattern chosen to play a part in such an apartment setting has to stand up to and outshine some pretty vibrant competition. Yet the latest of the large-scale, vivid abstract florals are well up to the task. By confining the floral design to only one part of the room, either on the walls, the curtains or the uphostery, the pattern is dramatic rather than overwhelming.

❖ **Look for:** technicolored, large-scale and boldly stylized all-over designs on brightly coloured backgrounds to provide the desired impact.

GLOBAL

The whole world is literally your inspiration and your market place when it comes to putting together a global-style room from a richly diverse mix of hand-crafted fabrics and artefacts. With such a cosmopolitan background, it's hard to pinpoint a single floral style to represent the global look. Different native techniques, such as hand-printing and batik, produce very distinctive designs, typified by an exuberant use of colours and strong motifs.

❖ **Look for:** hand-printed designs with strong motifs, often combined with geometric shapes. The motifs are either packed on to brilliantly coloured backgrounds or well-separated on neutral ones.

SOFT MODERN

The sheer unfussiness of a soft modern layout seems like a complete contradiction of the traditional floral pattern's habitat. But a cautious, contained use of a crisp floral pattern, maybe in conjunction with a geometric trellis or stripe, in a blind and curtains against plain walls, brings a desirable freshness to a simply furnished room. Graphic rather than naturalistic floral motifs, scattered across a neutral background, suit the simplicity of this style best.

❖ **Look for:** medium to large scale, colourful, open, stylized floral patterns with plenty of pale background showing.

ROMANTIC

Flowers are regularly sent and received as tributes of affection, and are an accepted currency of romance. So it follows that romantic room schemes offer the perfect opportunity for using floral patterns. The romantic floral style is pretty and feminine with clear, fairly realistic floral motifs in lively pastel shades. The medium-sized patterns sprawl over the fabric or wallpaper, often with ribbons and bows weaving through the design.

❖ **Look for:** all-over medium florals - especially patterns with roses in them - in pretty pastel colours on white or pale backgrounds.

GLAMOUR

There's certainly nothing shy or retiring about going for glamour as your favoured decorating look; it is the most ornate of any room style. If ever there was the perfect excuse for using masses of large-scale floral fabrics, it is the extravagance of a chic, glamorous approach to home design. The patterns rely on a range of tones rather than different colours for their effect. Saturation coverge with a floral brocade in a luxurious window treatment and dressy upholstery captures the perfect degree of theatricality.

❖ **Look for:** flamboyant two-toned or self-coloured damasks and brocades, or soft-focus floral designs on sheeny fabrics in pastel or dusky colours.

MEDITERRANEAN

The Provençal-inspired version of the Mediterranean look is practically defined by the traditional local prints. These are instantly recognizable by their busy mini and midi-scale patterns, with flower-derived motifs on white or primary coloured backgrounds. The freshness and jolity of the fabrics is well suited to informal settings and sunny situations.

❖ **Look for:** multicoloured, jaunty floral motifs closely packed on a vivid, contrasting background.

VICTORIAN

When you want a room to have a lovely, old-fashioned feel about it you can hardly improve on the extravagant, flowery look of the Victorian style. The look is deliberately ornate and cosy; the Victorians loved putting layer upon layer of densely patterned florals of all sizes, often in strong, rich colours as well as prettier pastels, on fabrics and wallpapers. This rosy living room scene is typical of the Victorian pleasure in elaborate detail and a confusion of pattern on upholstery, floors and accessories.

❖ **Look for:** richly coloured, compact flora designs on dark or intensely coloured backgrounds. Heavy, self-coloured velours and flock wallpapers are also ideal.

TOWN HOUSE

As a sophisticated, quintessentially English style, in which the country-cottage look is brought into an urban setting, the town house style relies heavily on floral patterns to establish the look. Traditionally, large and medium florals appear in partnership on the fabrics of curtains, upholstery and bedcovers, or as wallpaper on the walls of an elegant town house dining room. Old-fashioned chintzes usually depict very realistic roses, parrot tulips, peonies, lilies and wild flowers. Full-length curtains and bed drapes show off these richly colourful florals to best advantage.

❖ **Look for:** formal, well-organized designs with carefully worked motifs in natural colours, often arranged in columns or in conjunction with a stripe, on an elegant cream or coloured background.

PATTERNS THAT WORK

Since pattern juggling is the in-thing in home design, it pays to understand exactly what scale, colour and type of patterns will look right in relation to the size and style of the room you're decorating.

These days, all well dressed homes are wearing a lively assortment of the latest floral, striped, checked, paisley and country patterns. Such designs are the most flexible and helpful tools at your disposal when you are decorating your home, and inspire some of the brightest and best ideas.

A creative use of pattern can liven up a room, form a focal point or cover a flaw. Introducing a new pattern to a scheme can instantly change the character of a room. Interesting patterns also compensate for an absence of architectural detail on walls and ceilings in many modern houses, and help to make up for the lack of an attractive view when you live in a built-up area.

Your personal use of pattern virtually guarantees you an individual and stylish home. It doesn't matter if you opt for a single pattern or mix lots of different ones, feature them in small amounts on cushions, wallpaper borders or tiles, or over much larger areas as wallcoverings, carpets or upholstery. The real art of displaying pattern effectively lies in marrying different designs and colours with a sense of humour and perspective. Your aim is to make sure that any pattern you use works in relation to the size and style of the room.

High windows show off a large pattern at its best. The simplicity of stripe on the armchair and the checked swags and tails provide a refreshing contrast to the grandeur of the curtains.

SIZING UP PATTERNS

The 'oh what a lovely' fabric and the 'that'll look great in my living room' wallpaper are usually picked on the strength of their patterns alone, rather than with any visual effects in mind. Yet if you choose the scale and colour of the designs you use with care, a pattern can do much more for the image of a room than just look good.

In practice, each pattern must be seen in relation to the size of the room – or window or piece of furniture – it will be decorating. Generally, the height of the room, rather than its overall size, governs the scale of pattern it is best to choose for the walls. Large designs can be wasted on the walls of a small room, while the details of a mini-print will be lost in a spacious one.

When you are unsure about the most appropriate size of pattern to use, it is better to err on the large side, because this at least has the advantage of looking distinctive. Then smaller scale versions or spin-offs of large patterns on walls or curtains come in handy for creating a change of pace when used on upholstery and accessories.

Checkpoints

With their clean-cut and upbeat image, checks stand out, even in a crowd of patterns. For impact, the scale of the checks is changed to correspond to the size of the item they're associated with. So enormous checks prove an equal match for a magnificent bed (far right), while medium sized checks on an armchair (right) show up well against vibrantly patterned curtains.

Subtler results are achieved by altering the size of the checks to reflect their intended significance in the room. A smaller check (centre right) is used as curtains over a large window to make sure it's reasonably unobtrusive.

◨ Bring into line

All these blue and white stripes are perfect team mates. Those on the sofa are scaled down versions of the broader ones on the wall, as befits the smaller areas they cover.

Floral arrangements

There is a floral pattern to suit every situation, from tiny sprigs to all-over designs and big showy florals. A good way to judge the upshot of using these different sized floral designs is to see them covering similar scale seating like this.

Evidently as the designs get bigger, their visual impact on the room increases. So while the small floral motif on the armchair (above) looks pretty but modest, and the all-over flowery design on the sofa (above right) makes a brave splash, the giant sunflower pattern over the sofa (right) steals the show. Centring the motif on the cushions heightens the effect.

A SENSE OF PROPORTION

You can change, even enhance, the apparent proportions of a room according to the type of pattern you choose. The colour, arrangement and size of a design have a significant bearing on the impact it has on a room. Familiar patterns like checks, stripes and florals are constantly being updated to different scales and fashionable colourways to vary their effects.

Vertical stripes, painted or papered on the wall, for example, exaggerate the height of a lofty room, and are useful for making a room with a low ceiling look higher. In the same way, vertical striped curtains at a window make it seem taller.

In contrast, horizontal stripes make a room appear longer or wider than it really is. This effect has advantages when you want to add extra length or width to a small room, but is best avoided in a long corridor or hallway.

Bold or dark designs make the walls appear nearer, either overwhelming a small room or making it seem rather claustrophobic. On the other hand, a bright, flamboyant pattern makes a large room appear more welcoming.

Pale mini-prints and spriggy patterns create the impression that the walls are receding, so that a small room looks larger. From a distance or in a large room, the details of a fine pattern merge into one another and register as a single colour.

Spacial awareness
A shrewd use of pattern can alter the visible dimensions of a room. Compare the effects of similar floral designs on two bedroom walls. The spriggy wallpaper (above) appears to open up a small room so that it feels fresh and bright. A bolder, darker floral (left) seems to close in on the room for a more intimate effect.

Both pattern types have their uses when you want to make a room seem either bigger or more homely.

All in the background

Sometimes the arrangement of the individual motifs in a pattern counts more than their size or even their colour. Here two similar motifs on pale backgrounds behave completely differently according to their spacing. The far apart pattern looks bright and airy, while the closed up design seems stronger and cosier.

◨ Visual trickery

Clever positioning of patterns alters the apparent dimensions of a room. In this living room, both sets of stripes – vertically on the walls and horizontally on the sofa – exaggerate its proportions.

The tightly pleated folds in the curtains collaborate with the striped wallpaper in making the ceiling look higher than it really is. The horizontal stripes not only emphasize the length of the sofa but also redress the vertical trend by seeming to extend the width of the bay.

Pattern Scheming

Decide at the outset what sort of effect you are aiming for in your use of pattern – whether it is to serve as a general background, to pick out a favourite sofa or draw attention to a handsome window, or create a well planned blend of colours and designs throughout the room.

If in doubt about using patterns, start by introducing a single design into a plain scheme, and live with that alone for a while. You may want to stop there, or add more patterns.

Even when you're mixing patterns with a free hand, take care not to go overboard. Save boisterous patterns for walls and curtains, or the upholstery and carpet; it rarely works satisfactorily to have them in all places at once.

Accumulating patterns

Introducing small amounts of a single pattern into a plain room can be just as effective as using several large areas of coordinated patterns, or combining lots of different designs and colours in a complex scheme.

THEME PATTERNS

Establishing a theme in your decorating is great fun and a superb way of conveying the mood or look you want. You can create any effect, from the classical to the comically cartoon.

P atterns are a great way to give your home interest and colour. Why not go one better than safe stripes or checks, and give your room real character and individuality with a strongly themed pattern?

A good way to start is to pick on a design to suit the purpose of the room. Try a fresh vegetable print for a kitchen, or an all over pattern of cups and saucers in a dining room. Alternatively, let a print with a strong theme serve as an inspiration for an entire room. A high-backed wing chair covered in a heraldic tapestry-style fabric depicting a lion and a unicorn sets the tone for a neo-gothic living room scheme. Or use Toile de Jouy paper with capering shepherdesses on walls and ceiling as the basis for a romantic bedroom.

The following pages show just a few of the exciting theme pattern ideas available to spark your imagination.

Charming blue and white flowerpots are one fresh example of a popular ceramic theme for patterns. Other designs feature plates, teacups and saucers, urns, bowls and ginger jars and look good at a window or on a wall in a kitchen or dining room.

FRUIT FULL

There's enough fruit and vegetables to fill a market stall on current ranges of fabrics, wallpapers and tiles. You have the choice of everything from realistic looking marrows, cabbages and aubergines printed across a crisp white background to more flamboyant versions, with stylized vegetables arranged in highly colourful fashion. Such patterns look spectacular in a kitchen as curtains or blinds, or on the wall between cupboards – where all you want is a splash of bright colour over a small area.

Fruit is a popular theme, symbolic of health and vitality. Intertwined with vines and flowers, they provide such a richness of pattern and colour it's hard to imagine a better theme for an elegant dining room.

BERIBBONED

Flowing ribbons set with bows have been popular motifs for centuries, probably stemming from the time when they were given as tokens of a lady's favour to an honoured knight in medieval jousting tournaments. They retain a sweetly feminine image, and serve to add a softening aspect to more geometric all over patterns such as spots and checks. A pretty confection of flowers intertwined with ribbons makes unashamedly feminine bedlinen. Ribbons are often trained into flowing streamers or woven into trellis patterns, interspersed with bows or flowers on wallpaper borders.

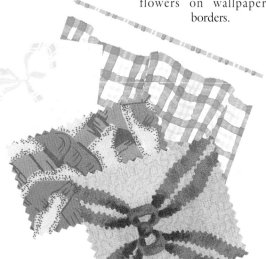

ANIMAL MAGIC

The animal kingdom in all its infinite variety is a popular source of fabric and paper designs. Animals feature prominently on brilliantly patterned fabrics as graceful cats or witty frogs – even brightly coloured insects – adding a touch of style and colour to a kitchen or bathroom. For a more exotic, regal touch, majestic elephants wander across fabrics, creating a strongly Eastern flavour.

The farmyard and countryside are unending sources of inspiration for a wide range of motifs and patterns. Fluffy rabbits, waddling ducks and strutting cockerels abound – from the gaily fanciful for children's rooms, to more realistic interpretations of the theme with swooping swallows and handsome pheasants.

Lovable animal cartoon characters have joined the ranks of their real-life counterparts as favourites for children's rooms. You can find many of them on coordinated bedlinen and wallpapers.

CELESTIAL BODIES

Stars of every shape and size have recently burst upon the interior design scene in shimmering splendour, with a galaxy of suns and moons in attendance. You can plan a bedroom so that as you lie in bed you are contemplating golden moons and planets spinning through a star-spangled, velvety sky.

Wallpapers have gone extraterrestrial with clusters of gold stars proliferating on dark blue backgrounds. They are perfect for decorating dramatic hallways and moody dining rooms. Team them with thematic objects such as pierced brass lanterns and astrological charts in ornate gilded frames.

Fabrics are just as star struck. Floating voiles printed with gold or silver stars are a wonderful way to dress a window or four-poster bed. Stars, moons and planets feature on printed and woven designs, twinkling with a light-catching metallic gleam. When draping starry fabrics, follow the theme through to the ends of the curtain poles by adding star or moon finials.

HERALDIC SPLENDOUR

Medieval Europe is faithfully evoked by heraldic prints and rich tapestry weaves. There are lions rampant, mythical griffins and unicorns, and deer at bay as well as the more geometric fleur-de-lys patterns. Work the stately patterns and luxurious colours against rugged iron furniture and beeswax candles for an up-to-the minute version of the Gothic style.

Think on a grand scale when using these fabrics in elaborate bed trimmings and window treatments. Drape a modern iron bedstead with natural cotton voile sporting stylized deer and rabbits. Or, for a touch of regal grandeur, fling a tapestry throw bearing a prancing unicorn across a bed or sofa.

COUNTRY IDYLL

The finely drawn and distinctive scenes on Toile de Jouy fabrics feature romantic interpretations of country life – shepherd boys minding their sheep, dainty milkmaids on woodland swings and so forth. The patterns are typically printed in a single colour on natural cream calico or linen. Traditionally printed in blue or pink, green and black versions have recently come to the fore as well. The delicate quality of the images conjures up a mellow, period look.

The idea dates back to eighteenth century France, when rich nobles and royalty loved to play at the simple rural life that they imagined was the peasants' lot. The style became very popular and expanded to depict musical instruments, sailing ships in harbour, hot air balloons drifting over meadows, portraits of court nobility and other scenes of eighteenth century life.

Today, wallpapers printed with the same designs make it simpler to recreate the unbroken pastoral idyll. Bare floorboards or fibre matting muster an authentic period feel in a living room or bedroom. Smother the bed in lacy pillows and bolsters to recapture the original feeling of opulence.

Used in smaller quantities, as living room curtains, for example, the designs mix well with simple stripes and checks. Although the patterns are often quite large, they still work well in small rooms, as the cream background and delicate lines are airy and light.

JUNGLE EFFECTS

Go wild in your own home with dazzling tiger or zebra stripes, or leopard and ocelot spots without harming a single paw or hoof of these elegant and beautiful creatures. The ultimately wild, back-to-nature look of real skins is superseded by fun fur fabrics – inspired by animal markings but which don't try too hard to mimic the real thing. Go for a tribal look by combining a chair covered in a sleek fur fabric with roughly carved furniture, ethnic baskets and other artefacts.

Nature's ingenious camouflage designs are inspiring a new range of abstract designs in wilder than wild colours. Use them for a funky, modern feel in curtains, upholstery and wallcoverings.

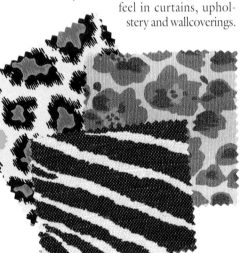

CLASSICAL

The graceful lines of classical architecture and decoration provide another strong design theme. Boldly elegant, yet perfectly balanced and engineered, the architecture of the ancient Greek and Roman empires has been copied down the ages and is still a design inspiration.

You can find fluted columns, vigorously sculpted torsos and whole facades printed on cream or white calico in tones of black or grey. These create a classically graceful yet coolly modern interior. Use these designs for a single curtain looped elegantly to one side with a thick black rope to enhance a stylish entrance hall, or in a bathroom with a black and white tiled floor and ochre rubbed walls.

TEXTURE IN DESIGN

*Mixing a good balance of rough, matt surfaces with smooth,
shiny ones around your home looks extremely stylish and adds enormously
to the visual interest of each room.*

The balance of textures in a decorating scheme is as important as the balance of colours and tones. Just as you blend and contrast colours with care, so you need to consider including a good mixture of textures – rough with smooth, matt with shiny, soft with hard – over the various surfaces in the room.

To some extent, this happens almost as a matter of course as you decorate and furnish a room – matt walls, glossy woodwork, soft carpet and a mixture of wood, metal and glass furniture all collaborate in the overall impression.

Accessories play their part, too, in introducing contrasting textures to a scheme. Consider the effect of fluffy towels set against shiny glazed tiles, a mirror against an ornately moulded frame or tapestry cushions scattered on a glossy leather sofa.

Despite having very little colour definition, this room still has a lively feel which is generated by a variety of different textures in the knobbly carpet, smooth curtains, wicker chair and unusual fabric on the sofa.

THINKING TEXTURE

To understand the qualities of different textures, it helps to draw up a list of rough versus smooth, matt as opposed to shiny and soft or hard materials and surfaces. Walk round your home placing each surface in one of the groups. You could end up with two lists that are something like this:

Rough/matt	Smooth/shiny
plaster	glass
wicker	ceramic tiles
sisal flooring	mirrors
towelling	laminates
untreated wood	polished wood
stone/slate	marble
damask	glazed cotton
hessian, linen	chrome, brass,
unglazed	polished leather
terracotta	gloss paint

If you also made categories for soft and hard textures, the list would be even longer.

A varied mix of all these textures is generally stimulating and satisfying, but professional designers often deliberately set out to emphasize one particular quality for maximum effect. One look they go for is a glittering metallic effect to reflect light from every surface around the room, or lots of rough matt surfaces for a more rugged, rustic feel.

◣ Tough stuff
Roughness prevails in this rustic kitchen, with iron hinges on the cupboard doors adding a tough, hard element to contrast with warmer wooden furniture and sisal flooring.

◂ Painted texture
Broken colour paint treatments like colour washing and ragging are often referred to as textured paint effects. Certainly the mottled paint finishes on the walls, fireplace and frame in this room give the impression of a gentle roughness. Note how the mirror, glazed ceramics on the mantelpiece and glass table top supply diverting areas of shine.

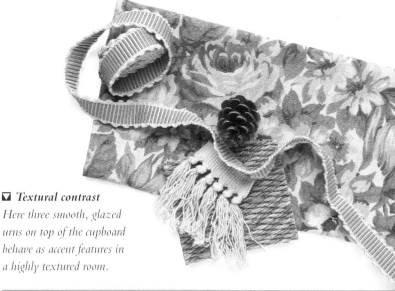

MOSTLY ROUGH

The latest trends in interior design concentrate on creating clever
contrasts between rugged and sleek. Modern homes counter-
balance bare brick walls with spindly steel lamps, flat-coloured
expanses of rough plaster with ornate gilt framed mirrors or a
knobbly woven twig coaster on a glass table top.

   You can often add an aspect of textural surprise to a room with
only one or two small touches. The room comes alive just as if you
had added a few brightly coloured cushions. Look around the
room and identify the missing texture, if any; perhaps there are too
few soft matt surfaces when the fabrics in curtains, upholstery and
cushions plus carpets are taken into consideration. Try placing a
glass table on natural fibre matting, for example, to contribute that
vital change of texture to a room.

◀ **Rough comfort**
*A tapestry weave chair filled with cushions is a delight to
the senses of touch and sight. The bouclé and needlepoint
textures are set off by the chunky detail of spindle fringing.*

MAINLY SMOOTH

Each area of your home has its own particular function and, to a certain extent, this determines the type of surfaces you use. Bathrooms and kitchen, where the emphasis is on cleanliness, hygiene and practicality, call for a high proportion of smooth, easily cleaned surfaces such as laminates, tiles, vinyl, glass and metal.

You can balance the cold, clinical effect of these hard, slick surfaces by adding natural wooden bowls, rough stoneware pots and coarse linen teatowels in the kitchen; or stacks of soft towels, a small rush-seated chair and a pyramid of natural sponges in a cane basket for a bathroom.

PRACTICAL MIXTURES

Living rooms need to feel comfortable and relaxing while being tough enough to stand up to the rigours of everyday use, and embodying the character of the home with pictures, photos and personal touches. Since the main aim is comfort, soft matt finishes such as textured, broken colour paint effects, damask curtains and velvety cushions are the strongest textural theme. But for contrast add rough jute flooring, or glossy wood floorboards with a scattering of tapestry rugs, a shiny mirror in a polished wood or hammered steel frame, or crisp paper lampshades.

You want to relax in a bedroom too, so soft comforting textures are winners. Indulge in airy voile drapes, plump quilting, silk and satin bolsters to provide contrasting finishes. But a modern polished steel four poster makes a wonderful foil for soft muslin or rich brocade hangings alike – the dissimilarity of the soft against the hard and shiny is exciting and unexpected.

In the dining room, prolonged hours of sitting around are unlikely so you can afford to concentrate on the theatrical effect of the room without sacrificing too much comfort. Use dark, matt wallcoverings, carpets and fabrics. To heighten the dramatic effect, set the table with glittering cutlery and glass as contrast.

▲ Glittering flash
The gleam of a polished wooden table acts as a foil for a glistening display of silver, glass and crystal. The creamy rose petals provide a soft contrast.

◀ Sheeny fabrics
Gold metallic thread in the cushion fabric represents an interesting combination of the soft and the shiny.

▲ Hygienically smooth
With the notable exception of the floor, every surface in this kitchen is silky smooth, from the dull gleam of the wooden unit doors to the glint of metal and glass in the table and chairs.

◀ Clean sweep
Even a bath towel can supply textural relief and richness in a ultra smooth setting. Here the eye is drawn to the plush towel hanging over the side of the bath as the only velvety element in this glossy bathroom.

TEXTURAL EFFECTS

Texture plays tricks with the senses – altering colours, creating reflections and stimulating touch. Rougher textures tend to soften a colour because the surface is broken up so that it doesn't reflect as much light. Smooth, glossy surfaces such as glazed tiles or shiny paintwork catch the light and project colours far more sharply. A certain colour – blue, for example – looks far brighter when used for gloss painting a door, than the same shade used as velvet curtains. Once aware of these textural elements and effects you can deliberately set up interesting and satisfying contrasts as the key to a distinctive layout.

▶ *Highly polished*
The high gloss kitchen units command attention for two reasons: their vivid colour and high sheen. The matt walls and natural woodwork counter the smooth effect.

▼ *Roughly rustic*
An abundance of roughened surfaces – rough plaster walls, natural fibres in the matting, chairs, rope and tassel tieback, plus textured paint effects – convey the impression of country chic.

COLOURFUL MAKE-OVERS

One of the quickest ways to breathe fresh life into a low-key colour scheme is by creating a new mood and style direction with colourful accent features and accessories.

A low-key or neutral colour scheme is sometimes the result of cautious planning rather than design. As you might expect, it seems to happen mostly when the intention is to create an easy-to-live-with setting by choosing furnishings and fabrics that do not tie you down to a set look. In an attempt to cover all eventualities, the final effect can sometimes end up looking characterless or just a little too safe.

Minor soft furnishings and accessories are usually the easiest and least expensive elements in a room to change. The details – lamps and pottery, together with simple window treatments and throws – provide the quickest way to introduce new colours that lead to a change of mood or style direction. The following pages show how to use these elements to inject a specific new modern or traditional look into a room.

The character of a room depends as much on a skilful use of colourful and distinctive accessories as it does on the basic furniture and soft furnishings.

117

CREATING A NEW LOOK

As the saying goes, 'a change is as good as a rest', meaning that a new look or setting refreshes flagging morale. The same is true of a familiar room scheme that you have

lived with for a few years. The fundamentals of a comfortable room – respectable furniture, carpet, curtains and ornaments – are in place, but they look rather dreary. You long to give the room a new image, yet it's hard to justify the expense of a total overhaul.

Even when you recognize that a room needs livening up, and know that you can make dramatic changes with a spot of nifty accessorizing, it's quite another matter to decide exactly what tack to take to give the room a fresher image.

One good thing about restyling a room with accessories is that you never have to go too far out on a colour, style or financial limb before you find out if you are

on the right track. You only need to find one or two items to distribute round the room to see if your ideas are going to work.

For inspiration you need look no further than the room itself. There are bound to be favoured items that you want to retain in your revised scheme; their colours or shapes are often useful pointers to a new theme.

It's vital to have an idea of how you want the room to look when you've rearranged it. The room on the left was treated to three make-overs – using a harmonious mix of zesty green and yellow for a fresh, modern look (below), concentrating on texture for a global style (right) and splashing out on vibrant, contrasting colours for a youthful, apartment image (overleaf).

To ensure that you end up with your chosen look, you must be consistent in your selection of shades, patterns and style of accessories. It's also important to position each item with precision, so that every accent colour and accessory makes its presence felt in the overall scheme.

◱ *Concentrating on textures*

A scan through the old room often reveals a direction finder for a new theme. Here, a global look evolved round two handsome metal urns, once hidden away in the wall unit. Two ethnic artefacts lead to others – woven bowls, wrought iron candleholders and a textured cotton throw. Together with rope trims and geometric patterns on a rug and a second pair of curtains hung over the plain ones, they establish the theme. In a scheme that relies on texture for interest, shiny metal objects, such as the urns and goblets, catch the eye as well as any brightly coloured accents.

◰ *Using harmonious colours*

Tangy green and yellow are a good, fresh choice for modernizing this room. They go well with the bottle green sofa and suit the clean lines and pared-down design of a contemporary look.

Faced with the original room, you can start by draping a vivid green throw over the settee. When you see its uplifting effect, you can go ahead and add other vibrant greens, as jaunty swags and tails over the window and plants and vases dotted round the room.

Although jollier, the scheme still lacks punch until you introduce the distinctive, zigzag standard lamp with its yellow shade. It is the linchpin for other yellow novelties and flowers that brighten up the room and helps to integrate the existing floral pottery into the new look.

BOLD COLOUR MOVES

Touches of over-the-top colour can miraculously transform the blandest of rooms. A maverick mix of coloured accessories can apply to the particular shades you choose, the variety of colours you use or to the amounts and the ways in which you distribute them in the room. A scattering of daring colours in a room can be just as eyecatching as a more comprehensive re-colour-scheming.

If you find that you enjoy revamping a room with accessories, you can easily make changeovers a seasonal exercise. That way, you can alter the colour scheming of your room to suit the prevailing climate and its associated lifestyle. In hot, summery weather you can live in open-air, cool colours, while on colder, wintery days you can enjoy rich, warming colours for cosiness.

◪ Colour and pattern combined

An alliance of strong colours and bold patterns is literally brilliant for giving a staid room an instantaneous boost. A length of blue and red plaid fabric draped as a swag with full-length tails at the window and a boldly striped, fringed throw on the settee is a youthful expedient for a quick or temporary change of looks. A mirror studded with coloured glass is a lucky find that complements the style and colour trends to perfection.

◪ The brightest contrasts

Originally, a coral-coloured lampshade and vase of carnations were the only hints of contrast colour in the room. When warmed up into a searing orange, flaring round the room from window to floor, the room becomes astoundingly jazzy. The purple throw, magazine holder and wicker basket chip in as rich supplementary dashes of contrast.

120

ROOM SCHEME CHECKLIST

The first step in a logical approach to planning the decorations of a room involves considering important details such as your family's likes and lifestyle as well as the merits and drawbacks of the room itself.

Arriving at a design for a room, complete with a clear image of its style, colour scheme, fabrics, flooring, lighting and accessories, is a satisfying exercise. Indeed, it is the essence of good design to reach a personalized scheme that caters for all your needs, activities, tastes and budget, while playing up the room's good points and taking on board existing items as well.

One of the most important principles of good design is practicality – the room should fulfil all the requirements you ask of it. Just like a professional interior designer interviewing a client, you need to ask yourself some penetrating questions that analyze your expectations of the room. In that way, you can reach a thorough understanding of how you intend to use the room and how the space itself suits the purpose, well in advance of thinking about specific colour schemes or room styles.

Later, you can use this information to give you a very basic feel for the look of the room. Then you can narrow down your choice of colour scheme, soft furnishings and accessories by collecting fabric, paper and paint swatches plus a scrap book of accessories that you assemble, together with a sketch of the room-to-be, on a sample board. Such meticulous preparation pays handsome dividends since you will eventually arrive at a design that is tailor-made to suit your personal requirements.

Time spent at the initial stage of planning a room is amply rewarded when you end up with an attractive and practical scheme that lives up to all your expectations for the space and the look.

PERSONAL QUESTIONNAIRE

Before you can decide on the style and mood of the room, there are a number of vital elements to be considered. Taking each of these factors in turn, ask yourself – and those you live with – the following questions, and make detailed notes of the answers. When you have completed the checklist, you can analyze how all the answers relate to one another, and begin to build up your summary or brief with an eye on your budget.

Thinking your plans through carefully at this stage avoids costly mistakes and helps you make the best use of the space available. The conclusions you reach are applied to all the later decisions about style, colour and pattern, so that the design of the room is built on your needs, rather than imposed on them.

FUNCTION

❖ **How will the room be used, by whom and at what time of the day?**
You're far more likely to come up with some practical solutions for decorating and furnishing a room when you take into consideration the role – or roles – it is called upon to play in the household. A bedroom may have to double as a playroom for younger children, for example, or a study for teenage children, or you may want a private, romantic and comfortable bed-sit retreat for yourself and your partner. A spare bedroom should be warm and welcoming, but but you can let rip with strong colours and zany ideas as nobody has to live with them for very long. Each different set of demands calls for a different approach to decorating and furnishing the rooms.

◀ *Multiple choice*
Where living space is at a premium, it pays to construct a bedroom scheme that leaves all your options open. Here, storage needs are anticipated by erecting shelves and a cupboard on the wall behind the bed to serve as a desk and a dressing table area as well as a place to keep belongings.

◀ Dinner party piece
When you use your dining room mostly for entertaining friends, decorating it in a dark midnight blue creates a moody, elegant setting that enhances the sense of occasion.

▶ On the look out
If you have a large window in your bathroom, why block out much of the light in the interests of privacy when you can hang long sheers that simply filter the light as they screen the window? You can install a blind behind to provide extra cover at night.

▶ In the light of day
Positioning a bed so that it catches the morning sunlight streaming in through an east-facing window is a wonderful way to greet a new day. As a concession to those who like to sleep on, the louvred shutters can cut out the glare.

LIGHT

❖ Which way does the room face – north or south?
The aspect of the room affects the type of light it receives. In the northern hemisphere, a north-facing room gets a cold, clear light, but if it faces south, it gets sunlight during most of the day, whereas an east-facing room gets direct light only in the morning. On a less positive note, the room may face another building or a large tree that blocks out much of the light and restricts the view. You can compensate for or distract attention from such negative features of the room in your planning.

Decide whether you want to maximize the natural light for a bright, airy feel, or perhaps screen out dazzling sunlight to create a diffused glow for a softer, cosier atmosphere. You can use colour and texture to reflect or absorb the amount of light in the room. For a bedroom, think about screening for privacy and shutting out light while you sleep.

❖ Do you have the right type of lighting in the right places for the purposes of the room?
There are many types of lighting available, and you can use these to create atmosphere as well as for practical purposes. Check the effect of daylight and artificial light on colour combinations – they can look very different.

❖ **Is the room large or small, long and narrow or boxy, high-ceilinged or low?**
Colours and patterns can work visual magic on architectural imperfections. A small room isn't necessarily a bar to strong colours and large patterns but they must be used carefully. You can visually stretch the height of a wall with striped wallpaper, or extend it horizontally with moulding, such as a dado rail. In a tiny room, a strong colour on the ceiling can help to balance a high ceiling.

❖ **Are there any interesting architectural features in the room?**
Tudor beams and leaded windows were a favourite feature of suburban houses of the 1930s. They may lead you towards heraldic prints or the rich glowing colours of the Arts and Crafts Movement; an Adam-style fireplace may start you off on a neo-classical theme. On the other hand, you may decide to play these down and focus on contemporary furniture and fabrics. You may have an awkward alcove you could turn into a study corner, or decide that the pure square shape of the room suggests Japanese minimalism.

◣ True to form
Often, when faced with a dominant structural feature in a room, like this large bay window with stained-glass insets, the best course of action is to play along with it. In this case, the coloured glass inspired the colour scheme of the soft furnishings, while the window treatment and the arrangement of the furniture reinforces the window's pivotal position in the room.

◪ Ugly duckling syndrome
Unusual but potentially awkward features can turn out to be the highlight of the room. Here, the odd-shaped window created when a large room with a huge bay window was divided into two separate rooms, is cleverly integrated into the bedroom. Fixing a dress curtain asymmetrically frames a charming group of furniture and pictures in the alcove, while blinds cover the windows.

❖ What items have to stay in the room?

When re-thinking the look of a room, it is very seldom that you can start from scratch. You usually have items you can't or don't want to change – a fairly new sofa, for example, or a brass bedstead, a favourite rug or picture. Flooring is often the last item to wear out, so you may also have to incorporate the existing carpet.

Such in situ items may be the starting point of a style decision, or the basis of a colour scheme. There are all sorts of cosmetic changes you can make with wallpaper, paint and fabrics – loose covering a sofa, wallpapering a fitted cupboard or adding a rug or two can work wonders at integrating a resident item into the new scheme.

▶ *Starting point*

A richly patterned rug can initiate an entire room scheme, from colour theme to layout. Too spectacular to be left on the floor, the colourful rug hangs in pride of place on one wall. An existing sofa is worked into the arrangement, courtesy of a tasselled throw and coordinating cushions.

▶ *Positive thinking*

At first sight, a low, beamed ceiling and uneven windows are a designer's nightmare. Yet a choice of pale colours produces a fresh room of great charm. Subtle tricks, such as raising the curtain pole over the French windows and hanging striped curtains, redress the imbalance between the two windows and apparently lift the ceiling.

ANALYZING YOUR BRIEF

When you have finished answering the questions, you should end up with a rough plan for the room. As a summary of your impressions and hopes, it serves as a reminder of the objectives to bear in mind as you come to styling decisions.

In looking at a revamp for a family room, for example, you may have come to several conclusions:

❖ You want the room to act as a cheerful, practical activity/television/dining room for the family, with scope to be neat and welcoming for guests.

❖ The family needs plenty of storage space.

❖ To fulfil the dual function, you need a flexible control of the natural light – maximum daylight for craft projects, plus dim-out for television viewing – along with localized artificial light sources in the evening to supply practical as well as atmospheric lighting.

❖ The woodstrip flooring is too good to hide under carpet.

❖ A dining table and chairs are a must for meals, homework and hobbies.

INTERPRETING THE RESULTS

You need to spend some time thinking through your observations and seeing how the different points relate to one another.

❖ The first two points combined suggest and anticipate that you need somewhere to stack away the family's activities – computer games and craft equipment for example – when visitors descend unannounced. A mix of open wooden shelving and low cupboards offers general and instant tidiness, while cupboard tops make excellent surfaces to place lamps and ornaments. If the cupboards are deep enough, you can even position the television so that you can slide a door across in front when it is not on to minimize distractions.

❖ When you're going to use the room for watching television during the day, it's worth fitting a roller blind or a cane blind at the window to screen out the sunshine. You can then add a pair of light curtains to draw across in the evening.

❖ The dining table could be wood to match the woodstrip flooring. Plenty of inexpensive, lightweight wicker chairs can provide versatile seating to go with it. And a rug can be used to differentiate between the living and activity/dining section of the room.

❖ Such an approach can readily accept a range of natural colours and materials in the shape of pot plants and ethnic artefacts.

Even at this stage, a germ of a global style for the room is emerging from your preliminary scrutiny. Based on reality and fact, you can go on and develop your ideas into your personalized room scheme.

❏ Made to order

The layout and furnishings of this multifunctional room meet most of the stipulations raised in the hypothetical family brief discussed on this page – there's plenty of living and dining space, a flexible seating plan, lots of adjustable light, both day and night, plus ample, stylish shelving and low cupboard storage.

Index

ACKNOWLEDGEMENTS

Photographs

7 Eaglemoss Publications/Ian Bagwell, 8 IPC /RHS, 8-9(c) Ken Kirkwood, 9 Eaglemoss Publications/Graham Rae, 9(t) Sanderson, 10 IPC Magazines/Robert Harding Syndication, 11 Sanderson, 12(t) Paul Ryan, 12(b) IPC Magazines/Robert Harding Syndication, 13-15 Eaglemoss Publications/Martin Chaffer, 16(t) Biggie Best, 16(b) IPC Magazines/Robert Harding Syndication, 17 Abode, 18(t) Laura Ashley, 18(b,r) IPC Magazines/Robert Harding Syndication, 18(br) Eaglemoss Publications/Graham Rae, 19(t) David Parmiter, 19(b) Paul Ryan, 20(tr) Laura Ashley, 20(c) Croydex Co, 20(bl) Eaglemoss Publications/Graham Rae, 20(br) Habitat, 21 IPC Magazines/Robert Harding Syndication, 22(tr) Harlequin, 22(br) Sue Atkinson, 22(bl) Crowson Fabrics, 23 Eaglemoss Publications/Graham Rae, 24(t) Coloroll, 24(b) EWA/Michael Dunne, 25(t) Abode, 25(bl) Eaglemoss Publications/Graham Rae, 25(br) IPC Magazines/Robert Harding Syndication, 26(t) IPC Magazines/Robert Harding Syndication, 26(bl) Eaglemoss Publications, 26-7(b) IPC Magazines/Robert Harding Syndication, 27(t) EWA/Spike Powell, 27(c) Sanderson, 27(b) Eaglemoss Publications/Graham Rae, 28(t,c) IPC Magazines/Robert Harding Syndication, 28(b) Robert Harding Picture Library, 29 Arcaid, 30(tl) EWA/Rodney Hyett, 30(b) PWA, 30-31(tc) Jane Churchill, 30-31(bc) Eaglemoss Publications/Paul Bricknell, 31(br) Abode, 32(tr) IPC Magazines/Robert Harding Syndication, 32(b) El Mueblé/RBA, 33(t) Crown, 33(bl) SIC/Beauffre/Deloffre, 33(br) Abode, 34(tl) Homeflair, 34(tr) Harlequin Fabrics, 34(bl) EWA/Rodney Hyett, 35-6 IPC Magazines/Robert Harding Syndication, 36-7 Jane Churchill, 36(b) EWA/Michael Dunne, 37(t) Eaglemoss Publications/Mark Wood, 37(c,b) IPC Magazines/Robert Harding Syndication, 38-9 IPC Magazines/Robert Harding Syndication, 38(bl) Habitat, 38(br), 39(t) IPC/RHL, 39(bl) Eaglemoss Publications/Mark Wood, 39(br) Habitat, 40 IPC Magazines/Robert Harding Syndication, 41 Ariadne, 42-3 Ariadne, 42(t) Dulux, 43(tr) Biggie Best, 43(b) Crown, 44(t) Dulux, 44(b) Ariadne, 45(t) EWA/Peter Wolosynski, 45(br) Croydex, 45(bl), 46(t) IPC

Magazines/Robert Harding Syndication, 46(b) EWA/David Giles, 47 Crowson Fabrics, 48(t) EWA/Spike Powell, 48(b) DoeHet Zelf, 49(t) IPC Magazines/Robert Har
ding Syndication, 49(bl) Eaglemoss Publications/Steve Tanner, 49(br) EWA/Peter Wolosynski, 50(tl) Eaglemoss Publications/Graham Rae, 50(tr) IPC Magazines/Robert Harding Syndication, 50(b) Ariadne, 51(t) EWA/Simon Upton, 51(b) Coloroll, 52(t) IPC Magazines/Robert Harding Syndication, 52(b) DoeHet Zelf, 53, 54(t) IPC Magazines/Robert Harding Syndication, 54(bl) Eaglemoss Publications/Graham Rae, 54(br) Paul Ryan, 55(t) EWA/Brian Harrison, 55(c) Eaglemoss Publications/Graham Rae, 55(b) EWA/Spike Powell, 56(t) IPC Magazines/Robert Harding Syndication, 56(b) Ariadne, 57(t)Tintawn Carpets, 57(b)Dulux, 58(tl) Habitat, 58(tr) IPC Magazines/Robert Harding Syndication, 58(b) Dulux, 59, 60, 61(t) IPC Magazines/Robert Harding Syndication, 61(b) Harlequin, 62-3 IPC Magazines/Robert Harding Syndication, 64(t) EWA/Di Lewis, 64(b) IPC Magazines/Robert Harding Syndication, 65 EWA/Rodney Hyett, 66-7(t) Christy Towels, 66-7(b) Habitat, 68-9(t) Paul Ryan, 68-9(bl) IPC Magazines/Robert Harding Syndication, 69(c,br) EWA/Michael Dunne, 70 Eaglemoss Publications/Simon Page-Ritchie, 71 Australian Interiors, 72 EWA/Spike Powell, 73(t) Laura Ashley, 73(b) EWA/Neil Lorimer, 74(t) EWA/Michael Dunne, 74(bl) Wickes, 74(br) Abode, 75(tl) Jonathan Pollock, 75(tr) Jane Churchill, 76(t) IPC Magazines/Robert Harding Syndication, 76(b) MFI, 77 Sanderson, 78(t) Ariadne, 78(b) Worldwide Syndication, 79(t) Habitat, 80(tl) Jonathan Pollock, 80(tr) IPC Magazines/Robert Harding Syndication, 80(b) Romo, 81 IPC Magazines/Robert Harding Syndication, 82-3(t) Ikea, 82-3(bl) IPC Magazines/Robert Harding Syndication, 83(c) IPC Magazines/Robert Harding Syndication, 83(tr) Boys Syndication, 83(bc) Eaglemoss Publications/Simon Page-Ritchie, 83(br) Eaglemoss Publications/Martin Chaffer, 84-5(tl) Habitat, 84(bl) IPC Magazines/Robert Harding Syndication, 85(tl) Monkwell, 85(br) Eaglemoss Publications/Simon Page-Ritchie, 86(t) Hill and Knowles, 86(cl) Eaglemoss Publications/Simon Page-Ritchie, 86(c,b) IPC Magazines/Robert Harding Syndication, 87 MCM/Christophe/Postic, 88-9(b) IWS Decorwool, 88(b)

Showerlux, 88-9(b) Lars Hallen/Design Press, 89(tr) MCM/Girardeau/Postic. 899(r) Paul Ryan, 90(cl) Laura Ashley, 90(bl) IPC Magazines/Robert Harding Syndication, 90-1(b) IPC Magazines/Robert Harding Syndication, 91(tr) Nursery Windows, 91(br) IPC Magazines/Robert Harding Syndication, 92(tl) Kaleidoscope, 92(bl) Romo, 92(cr) EWA/Di Lewis, 92(br) MC Idées/Chabaneix, 93, 94(t) Sanderson, 94(c) Eaglemoss Publications/Simon Page-Ritchie, 94(b), 95(t) IPC Magazines/Robert Harding Syndication, 95(c) Eaglemoss Publications/Simon Page-Ritchie, 95(b) Harlequin, 96(t) Interior Selection, 96(c) Eaglemoss Publications/Simon Page-Ritchie, 96(b) Vantona, 97(t) Crowson Fabrics, 97(c) Eaglemoss Publications/Simon Page-Ritchie, 97(b) Romo, 98(tl) PWA, 98(c) Eaglemoss Publications/Simon Page-Ritchie, 98(b) IPC Magazines/Robert Harding Syndication, 99 Laura Ashley, 100(t) Tintawn Carpets, 100(cl) Sanderson, 100(cr) Crowson, 100(b) Jane Churchill, 101(tl) Swish, 101(tr) Deptich Designs, 101(b) IPC Magazines/Robert Harding Syndication, 102(t) EWA/Spike Powell, 102(b), 103(t) IPC Magazines/Robert Harding Syndication, 103(b) EWA/Tim Beddow, 104(tl) Habitat, 104(tr) Jane Churchill, 104(b) Laura Ashley, 105 IPC Magazines/Robert Harding Syndication, 106(t) Jane Churchill, 106(b) Marks and Spencer, 107 IPC Magazines/Robert Harding Syndication, 108(l) Sheridan, 108-9(c) GCI London, 109(r) Laura Ashley, 110(t) Worldwide Syndication, 110(b) Marie Claire Maison, 111 Worldwide Syndication, 112-113 EWA/Simon Upton, 112(bl) Abode, 113(tr) Eaglemoss Publications/Graham Rae, 113(cr,bl) IPC Magazines/Robert Harding Syndication, 114 EWA/Neil Lorimer, 115(tl) Eaglemoss Publications/Simon Page-Ritchie, 115(tr,bl) IPC Magazines/Robert Harding Syndication, 115(br) Eaglemoss Publications/Graham Rae, 116(t) Miele, 116(b) IPC Magazines/Robert Harding Syndication, 117-120 Eaglemoss Publications/Graham Rae, 121 EWA/Neil Lorimer, 122(t) EWA/Jerry Tubby, 122(bl) Worldwide Syndication, 122-3(br) Paul Ryan, 123(t) IPC Magazines/Robert Harding Syndication, 124(t) EWA/Spike Powell, 124(b) IPC Magazines/Robert Harding Syndication, 125(t) EWA/Brian Harrison, 125(b) Ariadne, 126 Worldwide Syndication.